Seoultown Kitchen

Seoultown Kitchen

Korean Pub Grub to Share with Family and Friends

DEBBIE LEE

PHOTOGRAPHY BY QUENTIN BACON

KYLE BOOKS

Published in 2011 by Kyle Books
www.kylebooks.com

Distributed by National Book Network
4501 Forbes Blvd., Suite 200
Lanham, MD 20706
Phone: (800) 462-6420 Fax: (301) 429-5746
custserv@nbnbooks.com

Project editor: Anja Schmidt
Designer: Jacqui Caulton
Photographer: Quentin Bacon
Food Styling: Sienna De Govia
Prop Styling: Robin Turk
Copyeditor: Sarah Scheffel
Production: Lisa Pinnell and Gemma John

Library of Congress Control Number: 2011926471

Color reproduction by Fine Arts Repro House
Printed and bound in China by Toppan Leefung Printing Ltd

Contents

Introduction

You may remember me as the queen of Seoul 2 Soul from my stint on "The Next Food Network Star." I was the one creating cross-cultural concoctions from my life growing up as a Korean-American girl. Since my Korean roots have blessed me with such a wealth of inspiring food traditions and recipes, in my first cookbook, I've decided to share the richness of this very important half of my identity.

Growing up in the 1970s in Arizona, I thought I needed to hide my heritage and culture. In fact, I've spent most of my life trying to pretend not to be Korean. Like most second-generation Korean kids of immigrants, I battled with my identity, trying simultaneously to find myself and just be part of the crowd. It was not until my fortieth birthday, after my appearances on the Food Network show, that I truly embraced who I am and where I come from. Cooking on national television made me realize that my homeland was the source of some of the most amazing traditions, culture, and most of all food. The funny thing is, for years starting when I was a kid, when introducing myself to a group I would take Korean food with me, like *mandu* aka dumplings, as something to distinguish me. Nine out of ten times this method worked.

As I grew older and partook in all the amazing varieties of eateries that my heritage had to offer, I stumbled upon a wonderful daily ritual—a visit to the Korean drinking house, or pub, as most would call it. I got hooked after my first visit and started cooking my own versions of some K-town pub favorites. I also recognized the parallels between Korean pub fare and American bar food: fried snacks, hearty foods, anything on a stick. I had an epiphany—to share what I love to cook and eat.

My father tells me that I was blessed with the hand and spirit of my late grandmother, a talented cook who kept the best Korean food traditions alive in her new home. She could have been the Julia Child of Korea, he used to say. If it weren't for her teaching me through our special sign language (she didn't speak English and I didn't speak Korean), it may have been years before I tasted the goodness of a kimchee pancake or enjoyed the pleasures of cooking a roasted black cod. Gutsy and always looking to feed people—I do my best to carry her generous spirit with me each moment I breathe and cook.

History of the Korean Pub and the "Grub"

Contrary to most Americans' perceptions, there is so much more to Korean food and culture than the typical BBQ house and its beloved *galbee*, aka Korean short ribs. In Los Angeles alone, there are more than four thousand Korean restaurants and bars within a radius of a few miles, ranging from Korean BBQs to noodle houses, and, of course, the pop culture favorite, the *sool-jeep*, or pub. In fact, the *sool-jeep* is a daily stopover for Koreans as opposed to the BBQ house, which we reserve for special occasions.

The history of the *sool-jeep* dates back to at least the 1800s. My parents tell me that there were even different categories of the *sool-jeep*, and your ancestry (northern vs. southern) would dictate what kinds of *ahn-joo*, or snacks, would be available while you mingled with friends and co-workers. Back in my parents' days in Pyongyang (pre-war of course), my grandfather would always stop over at a local pub after work, enjoy a bottle of *Makgeolli*, our country's rice wine, and grab some snacks to tide him over before going home for the spread that my grandmother would prepare each night for dinner. The décor consisted of rustic wooden benches and tables, on which regulars would sometimes engrave their names, along with pots and pans hanging from the ceiling. There was always some air-brushed calligraphy spouting quotes to keep your spirits high. But what my grandfather remembers most about the *sool-jeep* was the food. The creature of habit that he was, he always ordered some kind of pancake (*jeon*), cold buckwheat noodles (*naeng-myun*), and pork belly—*bossam*-style, of course.

Similar to American neighborhood bars, the pub was the social scene for the Korean community, a place where everyone knew each other—basically your home away from home. Best of all—the food and drink was inexpensive. My grandfather believes that Koreans invented happy hour . . . an "hour" that lasted all day and night! To this day, whether in the heart of bustling Seoul or K-town in LA, you are bound to find hundreds of fashionistas, trend-setters, and taste-makers hanging out at one of the many popular *sool-jeeps*.

I have been known to frequent my favorite *sool-jeeps* several times a week. Nowadays, I've noticed the drink of choice is the traditional Korean *soju*, and *ahn-joo* has gone global—and that's no surprise to me. But Korean pub grub is still one of the best-kept secrets among Americans of Korean cuisine and culture . . . until now.

I hope that my modern take on Korean pub grub inspires you to cook, eat, drink, and share with family and friends. May this book bring culinary inspiration and new memories to you as it did to me. As my grandmother would say before starting a meal, "*MOK JA!*" (Eat and enjoy!)

Chapter One

Three Bites or Less: Skewers . . . and More Skewers

I don't think there is any country that does not have some sort of food on a stick. The concept is that you get to enjoy a variety of items on a skewer within a few bites. My mom tells me that, back in the day, my grandmother had an essential tool for parties and celebrations: a 3 x 3-foot iron griddle on which she would fry everything from kimchee to pancakes. She'd then put slices of fried kimchee and whatever else she had fried up on skewers for easy handling. I always knew my grams was a wise one!

A variety of skewers, sold per piece, are usually the first things listed on a Korean pub menu. Skewers are a great first course to get your taste buds going, so I've included a variety of delicious recipes here. When paired with a refreshing cocktail or hearty ale, they are sure to impress a crowd. Like my grams, I've kept things simple—three bites or less per skewer. Prep time is quick and cooking time is even quicker.

You can even invite your guests to become a part of the adventure and grill their own skewers, like at a Korean BBQ. Serve with trays of lettuce wraps and Korean pickles, and you have an easy summer buffet. This way, you get to spend more time mingling and drinking!

Bacon-wrapped Rice Cakes with a Jalapeño Ponzu

These rice cakes, or *tteok*, wrapped in bacon were a snack that my grandmother used to make for me. The rice cake lends it a chewy texture, while the crispy bacon adds smoky flavor. You can choose whatever bacon you like, just make sure the slices aren't too thick. The Jalapeño Ponzu melds perfectly with the salty sweetness of the pork. These can be assembled a day ahead and refrigerated until cooking time.

MAKES: 6 SKEWERS
PREP TIME: 30 MINUTES
COOK TIME: 10 MINUTES

For Skewers:

6 cylinder-shaped rice cakes, cut in half (see page 151)

1 tablespoon sesame oil

6 slices bacon, cut in half

For Jalapeño Ponzu:

1 cup soy sauce

¼ cup seasoned rice wine vinegar

2 tablespoons mirin

2 tablespoons granulated sugar

Juice of 2 oranges

Juice of 2 lemons

Juice of 2 limes

2 garlic cloves

1 jalapeño, slit in half, with seeds, plus 2 to 3 jalapeño rings, for garnish

1 tablespoon chopped chives, for garnish

1 tablespoon roasted and salted sesame seeds, for garnish

6 wooden skewers, soaked in cold water for 30 minutes

1 Drain and drizzle the rice cakes with the sesame oil to prevent them from sticking.

2 In a small stockpot, whisk together all ingredients for the ponzu and bring to a low boil for about 15 minutes. Drain in a cheesecloth or strainer and cool down in an ice bath. Place in a serving sauce dish and garnish with the jalapeño slices. Cover with plastic wrap and refrigerate until serving.

3 To assemble the skewers, take 1 piece of bacon and slice it in half vertically right down the middle. Wrap one half around each rice cake. Spear with a skewer, and repeat with the second half of the bacon to make 2 rice cakes per skewer.

4 Cook each skewer in a nonstick pan over medium-high heat for 4 to 5 minutes per side, or until the bacon is crispy and thoroughly cooked.

5 Transfer the skewers to a serving platter. Garnish with the chives and sesame seeds. Serve immediately with the Jalapeño Ponzu on the side.

Kimchee Citrus Pork with Roasted Fuji Apples

This is one of my favorite ways to eat pork. I love how the sweetness from the Fuji apple contrasts with the heat from the chiles in the kimchee. A touch of soy and citrus rounds out the flavors. It also can be transformed into an entrée: substitute whole pork chops for the pork loin cubes, and serve alongside a roasted apple for dinner. The skewers can be made a day ahead and refrigerated, and the kimchee can be storebought to save time.

MAKES: 8 SKEWERS
PREP TIME: 30 MINUTES
COOK TIME: 10 MINUTES

½ pound pork loin, cut into eight 1-inch cubes

1 tablespoon unsalted butter

1 large Fuji apple, peeled, cored, and sliced in half lengthwise

1 teaspoon granulated sugar

½ teaspoon cinnamon

Sea salt and white pepper to taste

For Kimchee Citrus Marinade:

¼ cup Classic Napa *Baechu* Kimchee (page 34)

¼ cup soy sauce

2 tablespoons seasoned rice wine vinegar

2 tablespoons orange juice

¼ cup sesame oil

Salt and white pepper to taste

1 tablespoon mint leaves, cut into a chiffonade, for garnish

8 wooden skewers, soaked in cold water for 30 minutes

1   Preheat the oven to 325°F.

2   In a food processor, combine all ingredients for the marinade except the sesame oil, salt, and white pepper. Blend well then whisk in the oil gradually. Season with salt and white pepper. Pour the marinade over the pork cubes in a medium bowl. Cover the bowl with plastic wrap and refrigerate for 30 minutes, or preferably overnight.

3   Grease a baking sheet with the butter and spread the apple slices on the sheet in a single layer. In a small bowl, combine the sugar and cinnamon, and sprinkle on top of the apples. Bake for 15 minutes, until the apples are firm but no longer crisp. Remove from the oven and let cool.

4   To assemble the skewers, cut the roasted apples into 1-inch cubes: You should have 16 cubes of apples and 8 cubes of marinated pork. On each skewer, alternate 1 cube apple with 1 cube pork, and then finish with 1 cube apple.

5   Preheat a seasoned grill or grill pan over medium-high heat until hot. Cook the skewers on each side for 3 to 4 minutes or until the pork is browned on the outside and just loses its pink color inside. Season with salt and white pepper. Transfer to a serving platter and garnish with the mint. Serve immediately.

Japanese Eggplant and Tofu with Pimento-Scallion Glaze

Two of my favorite things, coated in my favorite glaze . . . all on one skewer! Nothing is better than Japanese eggplant and tofu—the sweetness of the eggplant and the meatiness of the tofu is addicting. Add a brush of the Pimento-Scallion Glaze and you have perfection on a stick. This can also be re-imagined as a stir-fry, using the glaze as a sauce for the eggplant and tofu, tossed together in a hot wok.

MAKES: 8 SKEWERS
PREP TIME: 10 MINUTES
COOK TIME: 8 MINUTES

2 Japanese eggplants, cut into 16 rounds

½ package (8 ounces) extra-firm tofu, cut into eight 1-inch cubes

Salt and white pepper to taste

For Pimento-Scallion Glaze:

¼ cup red chile bean paste (*gochujang*)

3 tablespoons seasoned rice wine vinegar

3 tablespoons soy sauce

3 tablespoons mirin

3 tablespoons white sugar

2 teaspoons garlic powder

2 cloves garlic

¼ cup chopped scallions

¼ cup sesame oil

2 tablespoons chopped chives, for garnish

8 wooden skewers, soaked in cold water for 30 minutes

1 In a food processor, combine all ingredients for the glaze except the sesame oil. Blend well, then gradually incorporate the oil to emulsify the glaze. Transfer to a bowl and set aside.

2 Assemble each skewer, starting with an eggplant round, then a tofu cube, and then another eggplant round. Set aside.

3 Preheat a seasoned grill or grill pan over medium-high heat. Place the skewers on the grill and immediately brush with the Pimento-Scallion Glaze. Cook for 2 minutes, turn over, and brush the other side with the glaze; cook for 2 minutes more. Repeat on both sides for a total cooking time of 8 minutes. Season with salt and white pepper. Transfer to a serving platter and garnish with the chives. Serve immediately.

Salmon and Scallion Skewers with a Korean Miso-Honey Glaze

This is so simple, yet so delicious! Those who don't eat red meat will especially enjoy the succulent texture of the salmon paired with the miso-honey glaze. It calls for Korean miso, which is a bit stronger than the white Japanese version. The glaze keeps for at least 2 weeks, so you can utilize your leftovers on fish, poultry, and even pork chops.

MAKES: 8 SKEWERS
PREP TIME: 15 MINUTES
COOK TIME: 6 TO 8 MINUTES

1 pound salmon filet, cut into 8 rectangular chunks

8 scallions, white parts only, cut into sixteen ½-inch-long pieces

Sesame oil, for coating

Salt and white pepper to taste

For Korean Miso-Honey Glaze:

¼ cup Korean miso paste (*doenjang*)

¼ cup honey

3 tablespoons seasoned rice wine vinegar

2 tablespoons soy sauce

½ cup sesame oil

1 teaspoon black sesame seeds, for garnish

8 wooden skewers, soaked in cold water for 30 minutes

1 In a food processor, combine all ingredients for the glaze except the sesame oil. Blend well, then gradually incorporate the oil to emulsify the glaze. Transfer to a bowl and set aside.

2 Assemble each skewer starting with a piece of scallion, then a chunk of salmon, and then another piece of scallion. With a basting brush, lightly coat the salmon and scallions with sesame oil. Season with salt and white pepper.

3 Preheat a hot seasoned grill or grill pan over medium-high heat. Place the skewers on the grill and cook for 1 or 2 minutes; brush with the Korean Miso-Honey Glaze. Turnover, and brush on the other side with the glaze; cook for 1 to 2 minutes more. Repeat until the salmon turns opaque throughout, for a total cook time of 6 to 8 minutes.

4 Transfer to a serving platter and sprinkle with the black sesame seeds. Serve immediately.

Cremini Mushrooms and Pearl Onions with Sesame-Garlic Butter

The meaty texture of the cremini mushrooms and the sweetness of the pearl onions deliver the feeling of a grilled steak and onions without the beef. Even if you are a true carnivore, you will find yourself hooked on this vegetarian option. These skewers also make a great accompaniment to a perfectly grilled steak. The sesame-garlic butter really completes the flavor of two very bold and beautiful vegetables; it can be refrigerated for 2 weeks.

MAKES: 8 SKEWERS
PREP TIME: 20 MINUTES
COOK TIME: 5 MINUTES

8 pearl onions
16 cremini mushrooms, caps only
Salt and white pepper to taste

For Sesame-Garlic Butter:
4 tablespoons unsalted butter
2 tablespoons sesame oil
2 tablespoons minced fresh garlic
1 teaspoon roasted and salted sesame seeds

1 teaspoon black sesame seeds, for garnish
8 wooden skewers, soaked in cold water for 30 minutes

1   In a medium heat-resistant mixing bowl, pour ½ cup boiling water over the pearl onions. Wait a few minutes and then cool down by adding ice cubes to the water; drain in a colander. With a paring knife, gently remove the skins from the onions. Set the onions aside.

2   In a small saucepan, bring a pint of water to a high boil, and blanch the onions for 3 to 4 minutes, or until they are still firm but no longer crisp. Transfer to an ice bath to cool down; set aside.

3   Make the Sesame-Garlic Butter: In another small saucepan, melt the butter over very low heat. Add the sesame oil and then the garlic. Cook for 7 to 8 minutes, or until the garlic and sesame oil become very fragrant. Remove from the heat and add the sesame seeds. Transfer the butter mixture to a small mixing bowl and set aside.

4   Assemble each skewer, starting with a cremini mushroom cap, then a pearl onion, and another mushroom cap.

5   Preheat a seasoned grill or grill pan over medium-high heat. Place the skewers on the grill and immediately brush with some of the garlic butter, then season with salt and white pepper. Cook for 1 minute and turn over and repeat. Repeat 2 more times for a total cook time of 5 minutes. Transfer to a serving platter and sprinkle with the black sesame seeds. Serve immediately.

Pork Belly and Scallions

This is probably one of the simplest but tastiest skewers yet! The sweetness of the pork belly and the hint of scallion makes this the king of pork dishes! You can also throw this mixture into a buttered and toasted French roll with some mayo and tomatoes. You have now created the PLT (Pork Belly, Lettuce, and Tomato).

MAKES: 8 SKEWERS
PREP TIME: 5 MINUTES
COOK TIME: 10 MINUTES

1 piece pork belly, about 12 inches long and ½ inch thick

8 scallions, white parts only, cut in half

Sea salt and white pepper to taste

For Soy-Mirin Marinade:

¼ cup soy sauce

½ cup mirin

1 teaspoon black sesame seeds, for garnish

8 wooden skewers, soaked in cold water for 30 minutes

1   In a small bowl, whisk together the Soy-Mirin Marinade.

2   Slice the pork belly into 8 pieces. Place in a mixing bowl and pour the marinade on top. Season with salt and white pepper. Cover the bowl with plastic wrap and refrigerate for at least 30 minutes.

3   Once the meat has marinated, assemble the skewers: Start with a piece of scallion, then a piece of pork belly, and finish with another piece of scallion.

4   Preheat a seasoned grill or grill pan over medium-high heat. Place the skewers on the grill and sear on both sides for about 1½ minutes. Continue to cook, turning the skewers over every few minutes so that the meat and onion do not burn. When the pork belly has cooked to medium-well, season with salt, then take it off the grill to rest and finish cooking.

5   Transfer to a serving platter and garnish with the black sesame seeds. Serve immediately.

Spicy Chicken and Korean Peppers with Smoky Chile Rub

This is always a crowd pleaser on my food truck. The smoky flavor of the chile spice rub plus the heat of the pepper is perfect for those looking for an extra kick. See page 146 for the Korean pepper's attributes. You can substitute chicken thigh meat for a juicier dish. However, in L.A., it's all about the chicken breast!

MAKES: 8 SKEWERS
PREP TIME: 10 MINUTES
COOK TIME: 10 MINUTES

1 chicken breast (about ½ pound), cut into eight 1-inch cubes
6 large Korean peppers (*gochu*)
Sea salt to taste

For Smoky Chile Rub:
¼ cup finely ground chile powder, (*gochugaru*)
2 tablespoons smoked paprika
2 tablespoons granulated sugar
½ teaspoon garlic powder
½ teaspoon onion powder
½ teaspoon salt
¼ teaspoon black pepper
2 tablespoons soy sauce
¼ cup sesame oil

1 teaspoon white sesame seeds, for garnish
1 teaspoon black sesame seeds, for garnish
8 wooden skewers, soaked in cold water for 30 minutes

1 Make the Smoky Chile Rub: In a small mixing bowl, combine all the dry ingredients. Add the soy sauce and mix with a fork. Whisk in the olive and sesame oils. Pour half the rub over the chicken breast cubes in another bowl and toss to coat. Cover the bowl with plastic wrap and let the chicken marinate in the refrigerator for at least 1 hour.

2 Trim the tops and ends from the Korean peppers and cut into sixteen 1-inch-thick pieces. Set aside.

3 Once the chicken is marinated, assemble each skewer, starting with a piece of Korean pepper, then a piece of chicken, and finishing with another piece of Korean pepper.

4 Preheat a seasoned grill or grill pan over medium-high heat. Place the skewers on the grill and sear on both sides for 1½ minutes, then turn over and baste with the remaining rub. Continue to cook, turning the skewers over every few minutes so that the chicken and pepper do not burn. Season with salt. Transfer to a serving platter and sprinkle with white and black sesame seeds. Serve immediately.

Ginger-Soy Beef with Chile Tomatoes

This is an excellent choice for those who love Korean BBQ. Rib-eye steak always makes a juicy skewer since it has great marbling so it doesn't dry out when cooking. You can also use the marinade to prepare your favorite grilled meat or vegetable.

MAKES: 8 SKEWERS
PREP TIME: 15 MINUTES
COOK TIME: 10 MINUTES

1 pound rib-eye steak (about 1-inch thick), cut into 8 cubes

16 grape tomatoes

1 tablespoon finely ground chile powder (*gochugaru*)

1 teaspoon smoked paprika

1 tablespoon sesame oil

1 tablespoon olive oil

Salt and black pepper to taste

For Ginger-Soy Marinade:

½ yellow onion, cut in quarters

1 tablespoon minced fresh ginger

1 tablespoon minced fresh garlic

½ cup soy sauce

¼ cup brown sugar

¼ cup mirin

1 teaspoon garlic powder

1 teaspoon onion powder

½ teaspoon black pepper

¼ cup Coke or other cola

¼ cup sesame oil

2 tablespoons chopped scallions, green parts only, for garnish

8 wooden skewers, soaked in cold water for 30 minutes

1 Make the Ginger-Soy Marinade: In a food processor, mince the yellow onion. Add the ginger, garlic, soy sauce, brown sugar, mirin, and spices, and blend well. Transfer to a mixing bowl, add the cola, then whisk in the sesame oil to emulsify the marinade. Pour half of the marinade over the steak cubes in another mixing bowl. Cover the bowl with plastic wrap and refrigerate for 30 minutes.

2 In a third bowl, place the grape tomatoes, chile powder, smoked paprika, and sesame and olive oils. Toss well until the tomatoes are well coated. Season with salt and black pepper.

3 Once the meat is marinated, assemble each skewer, starting with a grape tomato, then a cube of steak, and finishing with another grape tomato.

4 Preheat a seasoned grill or grill pan over medium-high heat. Place the skewers on the grill and immediately brush with the marinade. Cook for 2 minutes, then turn over and brush the other side with the marinade. Repeat on both sides for a total cook time of 10 minutes, or until the steak is cooked to your desired doneness. Season with salt and black pepper. Transfer to a serving platter and garnish with the scallions. Serve immediately.

Chapter Two

Korean Pickles Five Ways: The Basics of Korean Pickling

What would the Korean people do without their pickles?! The Kosher dill pickle, we Americans know and love, but Koreans pickle everything from cucumbers to a hard-boiled eggs. My first memory of Korean food was watching my late grandmother make the pickles for the day. She pickled daikon, cucumbers, and even garlic cloves. I include recipes for all of these in this chapter.

Whenever we sit down for a meal, there are at least two or three different kinds of pickles on the table. Their acidity complements the sweet and spicy flavors of the various courses that my ancestors prepared. What's even better about Korean pickles is that they last for a few days, if not a week. They make tasty condiments for something as simple as a grilled steak or can even be tossed in a salad for added texture.

One thing to know about the Korean pickling: It's all about the salt. My grandmother always used finely ground sea salt. There is nothing quite like it—and I too have carried on this tradition in my kitchen. Don't forget to sterilize your jars in a hot-water bath or dishwater before filling them.

Here's to the pickle!

The Korean Pickle

This simple cucumber is probably the most classic of Korean pickles. It's what we refer to as *oy-zjie*. It is a very clean, yet very salty pickle. These are great to build upon and we actually make a seasoned vegetable salad, aka *namul*, out of these wonderful salty creatures. But the best way to appreciate the traditional Korean pickle is with a dab of *gochujang*, or Korean chile bean paste, and some warm rice. There's nothing like it . . .

MAKES: 12 PICKLES
PREP TIME: 5 MINUTES
COOK TIME: 10 MINUTES

12 pickling cucumbers, washed of any dirt
6 whole garlic cloves
3 tablespoons finely ground sea salt
1 quart plus 1 cup water
½ gallon glass jar with airtight lid

1 Place the cucumbers and garlic cloves in the jar. Set aside.

2 In a large stockpot, bring the water to a boil over medium-high heat. Add the salt and let simmer for a few minutes to create a brine.

3 Pour 1 cup of the brine at a time into the jar of cucumbers, leaving about 1 inch headspace at the top of the jar so the juices from the pickling process can occur.

4 Seal tightly with the lid and cover the top of the jar with a layer of plastic wrap to prevent air from coming in.

5 Place the jar in a dark cool space to ferment for 2 to 3 days. After the second day, taste a small piece of pickle. It should be soft like a traditional pickle, with a salty finish. If the pickle is still too crunchy, let it ferment for another day, or until it has reached the desired texture. You will also notice that the cucumber skins turn a yellowish color as the pickles ferment.

6 Serve immediately or refrigerate the pickles for up to 2 weeks.

Pickled Daikon

Pickled daikon is served as a refreshing condiment for one of the biggest sellers on my food truck—Korean fried chicken. I also love to chop it up and toss it in salads, noodles, even use it as a topping for a taco. Be sure to use Korean daikon, as it has a slightly sweeter texture and is a bit crisper than the Japanese daikon.

MAKES: 1 QUART
PREP TIME: 15 MINUTES
COOK TIME: 1 HOUR

1 Korean daikon, peeled and cut into 1-inch cubes

¼ cup salt

1 jalapeño, sliced into rings

3 whole garlic cloves

2 tablespoons minced ginger

2 tablespoons granulated sugar

6 cups Sprite or other lemon-lime soda

½ gallon glass jar with airtight lid

1 Place the daikon in a large mixing bowl and sprinkle with 2 tablespoons salt. Toss to coat well. Set aside for 30 minutes so the juices in the daikon are extracted. Rinse well with water, drain, and taste. The daikon should have a slightly salty finish. If not, coat the daikon with the remaining 2 tablespoons salt and set aside for another 30 minutes. The daikon should start to soften a bit, which will prep the vegetable for the picking process.

2 Place the daikon, jalapeño, garlic, ginger, sugar, and Sprite in the jar. Seal tightly with the lid and cover the top of the jar with plastic wrap to prevent air from coming in.

3 Place in a dark cool space to ferment for 2 to 3 days. After the second day, taste a piece. There should be an even balance of acid, as in a dill pickle, with a touch of sweetness. If the flavor is not fully developed, cover for another day and taste again. The length of the pickling process will vary depending upon weather and humidity conditions.

4 Serve immediately or refrigerate the pickles for up to 1 week.

Pickled Garlic Cloves

Garlic is probably one of the most predominant flavors in Korean cuisine. We use it in our pickles, marinades, and salads. We even eat the cloves as a snack. This condiment really brings out the sweetness of the garlic

MAKES: 1 QUART
PREP TIME: 5 MINUTES
COOK TIME: 15 MINUTES

1 quart plus 1 cup water

2 tablespoons finely ground sea salt

1 pound garlic cloves, peeled, tops trimmed and discarded

1 cup soy sauce

1½ cups seasoned rice wine vinegar

¼ cup sugar

1 cup Sprite or other lemon-lime soda

1 quart glass jar with airtight lid

1 In a medium saucepan over medium-high heat, bring the water to a rolling boil. Add the salt and simmer for about 5 minutes to create a brine.

2 Place the garlic cloves in a glass bowl and pour the hot brine over the garlic. Let stand for about 10 minutes. The garlic will start to cook in the heat of the brine. Drain and rinse well.

3 In a medium saucepan over medium heat, bring the soy sauce, rice vinegar, and sugar to a low boil. Remove from the heat and let stand for 5 minutes. Add the Sprite and mix with a spoon.

4 Place the garlic cloves in the jar and pour the liquid over. Seal tightly with the lid and wrap the top of the jar with plastic wrap to prevent air from coming in. Refrigerate the pickles for at least 1 day, if not 2 so they have time to cure. They will keep for 2 to 3 weeks, refrigerated.

Soy-Pickled Jalapeño Peppers

Among the best things to buy at a Korean supermarket are the soy-pickled jalapeño peppers that they sell at the *banchan* bar. *Banchan* are small side dishes for a Korean meal. Several of these sides can make an entrée. Whenever I frequent my favorite Korean BBQ restaurant in K-town, my friends always fill up on the *banchan* and forget there is an actual meal coming. Of all the *banchan* sides, I think these little soy-pickled peppers are the biggest crowd pleaser—not to mention highly addictive. They not only make a great condiment, but tasty toppers on burgers, sandwiches, and, my personal favorite . . . omelets.

MAKES: 1 CUP
PREP TIME: 10 MINUTES
COOK TIME: 10 MINUTES

8 jalapeños

3 garlic cloves, sliced paper thin

½ cup soy sauce

¾ cup seasoned rice wine vinegar

3 tablespoons granulated sugar,

2 tablespoons lime juice

1 tablespoons lemon juice

¼ cup Sprite or other lemon-lime soda

1 quart glass jar with airtight lid

1 On a cutting board, slice the jalapeños across to make thin rings, about ⅛ inch thick. If you desire a less spicy pickle dish, discard the seeds. Place the rings in the jar.

2 In a small saucepan over medium heat, bring the soy sauce, garlic cloves, rice vinegar, and sugar to a low boil for a few minutes to create a brine. Remove from the heat. Add the citrus juices and soda. Let sit for about 5 minutes to cool until warm.

3 Pour the warm brine over the jalapeños and tightly seal the jar with the lid. Cover the top of the jar with plastic wrap to prevent air from entering. Immediately refrigerate the pickles for at least 1 day and up to 2 weeks.

Spicy Pickled Cucumbers

If you are hankering for the essence of homemade kimchee but don't have enough time to make your own, these spicy pickled cucumbers will hit the spot. Known as a "quick kimchee," these garlicky and smoky babies are so full of flavor you may eat a whole bowl in one sitting! Typically these pickles are served at Korean BBQ houses as one of the *banchan* amenities. Persian cucumbers are thinner with less seeds than Mediterranean ones and are available at many upscale markets. These pickles taste better as they ferment and really take hold of the garlic and spices. Pour over a bowl of rice for an afternoon snack!

MAKES: 1 QUART
PREP TIME: 10 MINUTES
COOK TIME: 10 MINUTES

8 Persian cucumbers, washed of residue, cut into ¼-inch rounds

2 teaspoons finely ground sea salt

2 tablespoons minced garlic

2 teaspoons finely ground chile powder (*gochugaru*)

½ teaspoon garlic powder

½ teaspoon onion powder

2 tablespoons granulated sugar

¼ cup seasoned rice wine vinegar

2 tablespoons sesame oil

roasted and salted sesame seeds, for garnish

1 Place the cucumbers in a large mixing bowl. Sprinkle with the salt and toss well to coat. Set aside and let mixture stand for about 30 minutes so that a quick brining process occurs and the liquid from the cucumber starts to extract.

2 Rinse the cucumbers well and drain. Place in a dry bowl. Add the garlic, chile powder, garlic powder, onion powder, and sugar. Using a spoon or gloves, mix well to incorporate the spices. Add the vinegar and mix well.

3 Drizzle in the sesame oil and give the cucumbers one more good toss.

4 Place in an airtight container and cool in the refrigerator for at least 30 minutes to capture the full flavor essence. They will keep for 3 to 4 days.

Chapter Three

There's Never Enough Kimchee!

I think the most amazing bonding experience I had with my grandmother was that of learning how to make our country's staple, kimchee, in her kitchen. You could always find gallons of various types of kimchee in her fridge or outside fermenting in the sun. My grandmother would give me a little bowl and show me, using our quasi-sign language, how to make the perfect batch. I admit during my younger years I did not have the patience to truly appreciate the art of making this remarkable dish, as it does take some time. But once you savor the first bite of a homemade batch of kimchee, you will realize it was worth every drop of juice.

Kimchee, which is actually our standard pickle, is typically made from Napa cabbage or daikon seasoned with Korean chiles, garlic, onions, ginger, and some kind of fish agent to cure it. My family is of northern Korean descent and my grandmother maintained that the northern version is the original kimchee—it's a bit more gingery, a little more acidic, than the south Korean version and uses primarily baby salted shrimp for fermenting. After the war, my family fled to the south, where the climate was warmer and a bit more humid. My mother remembers the kimchee boiling and rotting so fast that they needed to add a sweet rice flour to the chile paste, and anchovies or oysters to stabilize the ingredients. In my opinion, the northern version has a much cleaner finish.

What is so great about kimchee is that there are so many variations. The most common is *baechu kimchee*, the Napa cabbage variety mentioned above, however, depending upon the season, we use everything from cucumber to daikon and even make a scallion kimchee. The contrast of the chile's heat and the vegetable's sweetness is so unique in kimchee that is now used as more than a condiment. You can chop it up to create a slaw, puree it for a marinade to use on fish or pork, or even smash it into your favorite rendition of mashed potatoes.

Classic Napa Baechu Kimchee

The most common type of kimchee used in stews, fried rice, and stir-frys, the flavors of the chile and garlic really seep into the cabbage over time. My favorite part are the wilted leaves, especially topped on a burger.

MAKES: 1 GALLON
PREP TIME: 20 MINUTES
COOK TIME: 1 HOUR

2 heads Napa cabbage, quartered lengthwise

1 cup finely ground sea salt

1 Korean daikon, peeled and grated

4 bunches scallions, julienned as thinly as possible

¼ cup minced garlic

2 tablespoons minced ginger

¼ cup coarse chile pepper flakes (*gochugaru*)

2 tablespoons baby salted shrimp (*saewoojut*)

1 gallon glass jar with an airtight lid

1 In a large mixing bowl, liberally sprinkle each layer of the cabbage leaves with half of the salt. Place each quarter with the outside facing down so that it resembles a boat. Set aside for about 45 minutes.

2 In a medium mixing bowl, combine the daikon, scallions, garlic, ginger, chile pepper flakes, and salted shrimp, tossing so that all items are well incorporated. Set aside.

3 Rinse each cabbage quarter with water, making sure to rinse between each layer of leaves to get rid of excess salt. Repeat step 1 using the remaining salt. The salting process softens the leaves.

4 Rinse the cabbage one more time then taste a small piece of cabbage leaf. You should be able to taste a very prominent saltiness, but if it is too salty, rinse with water one more time.

5 Take one cabbage quarter at a time and spread a little bit of the daikon mixture on each layer of cabbage leaves, making sure to work toward the core of the cabbage. Then, starting with the core side first, roll each quarter as if you are making a cabbage roll. Place in the jar, making sure to pack the cabbage rolls tightly. Seal tightly with the lid and then cover the top of the jar with plastic wrap to prevent air from entering.

6 Place in a dark cool place for 1 day. Remove the lid and turn the cabbage rolls in the jar so that the top cabbage goes to the bottom and vice-versa. This will allow the kimchee to ferment evenly. Seal the lid and re-wrap with plastic wrap. Place the jar in a cool dark place for another day.

7 Open the jar and taste a small piece of cabbage leaf to check for ripeness. The flavor should demonstrate a bit of acid. If the acid is not prevalent, then let the kimchee chill for one more day to ripen. Slice a cabbage roll one at a time for serving. They will keep for 10 days in the fridge.

Daikon Kimchee

This is by far my personal favorite kimchee. Daikon kimchee, or what we Koreans refer to as *ghak-du-ki*, is much more robust with chile and garlic than napa kimchee. The longer it ferments, the better it tastes. One of the most common ways we eat this kimchee is with a bone-marrow stock (page 148) in winter. We dip or wash the kimchee in the soup broth, melding all the flavors together. There's nothing else you need to add to this meal. Daikon kimchee is also delicious tossed with ramen or udon noodles. The flavor of the radish is so pronounced that it livens up any soup or broth.

MAKES: 1 GALLON
PREP TIME: 20 MINUTES
COOK TIME: 30 MINUTES

2 large Korean daikons, peeled and cut into 1-inch cubes, plus 1 Korean daikon, peeled and grated

½ cup finely ground sea salt

4 bunches scallions, julienned as thinly as possible

¼ cup minced garlic

2 tablespoons minced ginger

¼ cup coarse chile pepper flakes (*gochugaru*)

2 tablespoons baby salted shrimp (*saewoojut*)

1 gallon glass jar with an airtight lid

1 Place the daikon cubes in a large mixing bowl. Sprinkle with half of the salt and toss well. Set aside and let sit for about 30 minutes to extract the liquid from the daikon.

2 In a medium mixing bowl, combine the grated daikon, scallions, garlic, ginger, chile pepper flakes, and salted shrimp, tossing so that all the ingredients are well incorporated. Set aside.

3 Drain the daikon cubes in a colander and rinse well under cold water. Repeat step 1 using the remaining ¼ cup salt.

4 Rinse the daikon cubes one more time and taste one. You should be able to taste a very prominent saltiness. If it is too salty, rinse with water one more time.

5 Add the shrimp mixture to the daikon cubes in the large bowl and, with a wooden spoon, mix well to thoroughly coat the radish. Pour the entire mixture into the jar.

6 Seal tightly with the lid and then cover the top of the jar with plastic wrap to prevent air from entering. Place in a cool dark place for 1 day. Remove the lid and, with a wooden spoon, mix the daikon well, so that the radishes on top go to the bottom and vice-versa. This will allow the kimchee to ferment evenly. Seal tightly with the lid and rewrap with plastic wrap. Place the jar in a cool dark place for another day.

7 Open the jar and taste a small piece of the daikon to check for ripeness. The flavor should demonstrate a bit of acid from the fermentation process. If the acid is not prevalent, then let the kimchee sit for one more day to ripen. Place the jar in the refrigerator and let sit for one more day before serving. It will keep for up to 10 days in the fridge.

Water Kimchee

Another tempting summer treat, water kimchee, or *mul kimchee*, is also served with some of our spicier dishes as a cooling agent. You will normally find this sweet and refreshing dish at a tofu house. As opposed to some of the other kimchee recipes in this chapter, water kimchee is basically the juice of the kimchee. The ratio is 1 part radish to 3 parts liquid. You literally drink it from the bowl like you'd drink miso soup. As a kid, I used to sip this like a cold summer soup for an afternoon snack, with a bit of rice and seaweed on the side. It's refreshing and satisfying all in one gulp!

MAKES: 1 GALLON
PREP TIME: 10 MINUTES
COOK TIME: 10 MINUTES

2 large Korean daikon, peeled, quartered lengthwise, and sliced across $1/8$ of an inch thick
$1/4$ cup finely ground sea salt
$1/4$ cup minced garlic
2 tablespoons minced ginger
4 pimento peppers, sliced into rings about $1/8$ inch thick
3 tablespoons granulated sugar
1 gallon glass jar with airtight lid

1   Place the daikon in a large mixing bowl. Sprinkle with 2 tablespoons salt and toss well. Set aside and let sit for about 30 minutes to extract the liquid from the daikon.

2   Place the garlic, ginger, pimentos, and sugar in the jar. Set aside.

3   Rinse the daikon in a colander under cold water. Repeat step 1 and let sit for another 30 minutes. Rinse again.

4   Add the daikon to the canning jar and pour the cold water on top, leaving about 1 inch headspace from the lip of the jar.

5   Seal tightly with the lid and then cover the top of the jar with plastic wrap to prevent air from entering. Place in a dark cool place for 2 days. Remove the lid and taste a spoonful of the liquid. It should have a nice balance of salt and sweet, with a hint of ginger and acid. If the juice is not yet flavorful, cover again and let sit for another day.

6   Place the ripened kimchee in the refrigerator and let sit for one more day. Enjoy in a soup bowl with a little bit of the radish and a good amount of the liquid. This will keep for up to 10 days in the fridge.

Icicle Radish Kimchee

The sweetness and crunchy texture of these smaller daikon are to die for. And the best part of this kimchee is that you also get to eat the green tops of these little guys. Since the radishes are somewhat seasonal, we all would run to the table when my grandmother made this kimchee. It was a special event. This particular kimchee also has a unique salt taste to it, so when snacking on it, remember less is always more— as my mom would say. A little heartier than daikon kimchee, icicle radish kimchee is a natural pairing for grilled meats and some rice.

MAKES: 1 GALLON
PREP TIME: 20 MINUTES
COOK TIME: 20 MINUTES

4 bunches icicle radishes (available in Asian markets), washed of any dirt and green tops left intact

½ cup finely ground sea salt

1 Korean daikon, peeled and grated

4 bunches scallions, julienned as thinly as possible

¼ cup minced garlic

2 tablespoons minced ginger

¼ cup coarse chile pepper flakes (*gochugaru*)

2 tablespoons baby salted shrimp (*saewoojut*)

1 gallon glass jar with airtight lid

1 Place the radishes in a large mixing bowl. Sprinkle with ¼ cup salt and toss well. Set aside and let sit for about 30 minutes to extract the liquid from the radishes.

2 In a medium mixing bowl, combine the daikon, scallions, garlic, ginger, chile pepper flakes, and salted shrimp, tossing so that all the ingredients are well incorporated. Set aside.

3 Drain the radishes in a colander and rinse well under cold water. Repeat step 1 using the remaining ¼ cup salt.

4 Rinse the radishes one more time and taste one cube. You should be able to taste a very prominent saltiness. If it is too salty, rinse with water one more time. Place in a large mixing bowl.

5 Add half of the daikon mixture to the radishes and, with a wooden spoon, mix well to thoroughly coat the radishes. Pour the mixture into the canning jar and top with the remaining half of the daikon mixture.

6 Seal tightly with the lid and then cover the top of the jar with plastic wrap to prevent air from entering. Place in a dark cool place for 1 day. Remove the lid and, using tongs, turn over the radishes, so that the radishes on top go to the bottom and vice-versa. This will allow the kimchee to ripen evenly. Seal the lid and rewrap with plastic wrap. Place the jar in a cool dark place for another day.

7 Open the jar and taste a small piece of the radish to check for ripeness. The flavor should demonstrate a bit of acid and a bite of salt from the fermentation process. If the acid is not prevalent, then let the kimchee sit for one more day to ripen. Refrigerate for one more day before serving. This will keep for up to 10 days in the fridge.

Cucumber Kimchee

The refreshing flavors of this kimchee bring me back to the summer days of my childhood, when pickling cucumbers were at their best. My grandmother would make many jars at a time to give away to friends and neighbors. I would ask my grandmother to slice the cucumbers into spears so I could snack on them in the afternoon. This kimchee has a little more ginger flavor—feel free to modify according to your taste buds.

MAKES: 1 GALLON
PREP TIME: 20 MINUTES
COOK TIME: 30 MINUTES

12 pickling cucumbers, washed of any dirt

½ cup finely ground sea salt

1 Korean daikon, peeled and grated

4 bunches scallions, julienned as thinly as possible

¼ cup minced garlic

3 tablespoons minced ginger

¼ cup coarse chile pepper flakes (*gochugaru*)

2 tablespoons baby salted shrimp (*saewoojut*)

1 gallon glass jar with an airtight lid

1. Lay the cucumbers on a cutting board. With a paring knife, cut lengthwise to make a 2-inch slit in each cucumber. Flip them over and repeat on the other side. Transfer to a large mixing bowl, sprinkle with ¼ cup salt, and toss well. Set aside and let sit for about 30 minutes to extract the liquid from the cucumbers.

2. Meanwhile, in a medium mixing bowl, combine the daikon, scallions, garlic, ginger, chile pepper flakes, and salted shrimp, tossing so that all the ingredients are well incorporated. Set aside.

3. Rinse the cucumbers under cold water, making sure to get rid of any excess salt. With the remaining ¼ cup salt, repeat the salting, tossing, and setting aside per step 1.

4. Rinse the cucumbers one more time and slice off a small piece to taste. You should taste a very prominent saltiness, but if it is too salty, rinse with water one more time. Place in a large mixing bowl.

5. Stuff each cucumber with 2 tablespoons of the daikon mixture and place in the jar. Pour any remaining daikon mixture on top. Seal tightly with the lid and cover the top of the jar with plastic wrap to prevent air from entering. Place in a dark cool place for 1 day. Remove the lid and, using tongs, turn over the cucumbers, making sure to rotate the bottom one to the top and vice-versa, allowing the kimchee to ripen evenly. Seal the jar, rewrap in plastic, and place in a cool dark place for another day.

6. Open the jar and cut a small piece of the cucumber to check for ripeness. The flavor should demonstrate a bit of acid from the fermentation process. If the acid is not prevalent, then refrigerate the kimchee for another day to ripen. To serve, cut into spears. These keep for 10 days.

Chapter Four

Some Like It Cold . . .
Some Like It Hot!
Different Takes on the Noodle

Every culture I know has an affinity for some kind of noodles. It's one of the universal dishes that we can all relate to. Especially within the various Asian cultures, noodles are a regular part of our weekly menu. We eat them hot, cold, as an appetizer, and an entrée. What I love most about Korean cuisine is that our noodle dishes range from something cool and light for a hot day to something warm and hearty to cure a cold—or even a hangover. I love the noodle stories my mother used to share with me of her times as a child in Pyongyang, North Korea. Just hearing about the Spicy Chilled Buckwheat Noodles and Summer Buckwheat Noodles in Chilled Beef Broth served in my great grandfather's well-known noodle house made me hungry—and both are offered in this chapter.

Noodles offer a great sense of comfort. It's the first thing I crave when I'm sick or just wanting something to warm my tummy. Any Korean pub you walk into will have at least a few noodle dishes on the menu; we normally order one for the table. Whether spicy or served in a bowlful of flavorful broth, they are great polished off with an ice cold beer.

Spicy Chilled Buckwheat Noodles

Bibim naeng myun is a northern regional specialty. We eat these spicy cold noodles even when it's 8 degrees below zero. The spicy-sweet flavor of the Gochujang Vinaigrette along with the array of vegetables in my version of this nutty and chewy soba noodle dish is always satisfying. Traditionally we serve this dish with raw fish on top or sometimes even raw meat, like a tartare. I personally prefer this vegetarian version, as the sauce and noodles really become the star of the meal.

SERVES: 6
PREP TIME: 20 MINUTES
COOK TIME: 20 MINUTES

8 ounces buckwheat noodles (*naeng myun*), dried or frozen

3 tablespoons sesame oil

1 red onion, julienned

3 tablespoons seasoned rice wine vinegar

1 tablespoon granulated sugar

Salt and black pepper to taste

1 hot-house cucumber, julienned

1 Fuji apple, cored and julienned

2 carrots, julienned

For Gochujang Vinaigrette:

¼ cup red chile bean paste (*gochujang*)

3 tablespoons honey

¼ cup seasoned rice wine vinegar

2 tablespoons soy sauce

¼ cup sesame oil

3 eggs, boiled, peeled, and halved

¼ cup chopped scallions, green parts only, for garnish

1 In a large stockpot over medium-high heat, bring water with a pinch of salt to a boil. Add the noodles, stirring occasionally with tongs to make sure the noodles don't clump, and cook for 6 to 8 minutes if using dried noodles, and 4 to 5 minutes if using frozen or fresh. Immediately run under cold water, stirring with the tongs again to keep the noodles from clumping. Once the noodles are cool, drain, transfer to a medium mixing bowl, drizzle with the sesame oil, and toss so that noodles keep their elasticity. Set aside.

2 In a small mixing bowl, combine the red onion, rice wine vinegar, sugar, and a pinch of salt. Toss well and set aside.

3 In a food processor, combine all ingredients for the Gochujang Vinaigrette except the sesame oil and puree. Drizzle in the sesame oil, blending well to emulsify the vinaigrette. Return to the small mixing bowl and set aside.

4 In a large mixing bowl, combine the noodles, half of the cucumber, the apple and carrots, and half of the vinaigrette. Season with salt and pepper, and toss well, making sure to evenly distribute the ingredients. Mound in the middle of a large serving bowl or divide into 6 bowls. Drizzle with the additional dressing and top with the remaining cucumber and boiled eggs. Sprinkle with the scallions and serve immediately.

Kimchee Ramen

I don't know of any Korean who can live without eating ramen. It's in our blood. Especially during the winter months, we love our ramen noodles. We take this Japanese favorite and transform it into an extra-spicy version that can really aid in clearing the sinuses. A Korean pub staple to consume while drinking with your friends, ramen is also a popular after-school snack for kids as well as a midnight munchie meal. Try this recipe at home and see for yourself.

SERVES: 4
PREP TIME: 10 MINUTES
COOK TIME: 30 MINUTES

2 packages ramen noodles
(4.5 ounces each), dried or fresh

2 quarts Kimchee Broth (see below)

1 package fish cake tempura, sliced
(available in Asian markets)

1 cup Classic Napa Kimchee
(page 34), julienned

4 eggs, beaten

For Kimchee Broth:

6 cups Dashi Stock (page 147)

2 cups kimchee juice

3 tablespoons finely ground chile
powder (*gochugaru*)

2 tablespoons granulated sugar,

Sea salt and white pepper to taste

4 sheets roasted seaweed (*nori,*
available in Asian markets), for
garnish

1 First, make the Kimchee Broth: In a medium stockpot, bring the Dashi Stock and kimchee juice to a high boil. Reduce to a low simmer and add the chile powder and sugar. Season with salt and pepper. Simmer for 15 to 20 minutes to meld the flavors.

2 Return the broth to a rolling boil and add the ramen noodles to the pot. Boil for 4 to 5 minutes or until the noodles are tender. Add the fish cake tempura and kimchee, then add the eggs while the broth is still boiling, swirling the eggs with chopsticks and breaking them up as they rise to the surface. Remove from the heat immediately.

3 Divide the noodles between 4 large soup bowls. Add the broth, dividing evenly between the bowls. Crumble 1 sheet of seaweed on top of each serving. Serve immediately.

Seoulful Soba with Fried Tofu Steaks

Another dish we inherited from the Japanese, soba is a sweet buckwheat noodle. Traditionally if you would go to a Japanese noodle house, you would eat them plain with a soy-based dashi broth—or what we would refer to as soba sauce. Koreans tends to eat them in a hot soup broth or tossed with some kimchee and vegetables. I concocted a variation on a Seoul-style soba salad that has always been a hit for lunch or even as a side dish for a buffet when I used to cater. You can add some grilled steak or seafood to this dish, to make it a heartier meal. But my personal preference is fried tofu steaks.

SERVES: 6
PREP TIME: 20 MINUTES
COOK TIME: 20 MINUTES

2 bundles soba noodles, dried

½ cup soy sauce

¼ cup sesame oil

¼ cup mirin

One 16-ounce package extra-firm tofu, drained (see page 149)

Sea salt and white pepper to taste

2 tablespoons vegetable oil for frying

½ head red cabbage, julienned

1 cup bean sprouts

1 bunch scallions, white parts only, julienned

1 hot-house cucumber, julienned

2 Roma tomatoes, pulp and seeds removed, julienned

2 carrots, julienned

For Ginger-Cilantro Ponzu Dressing:

½ cup pickled ginger with juice

1 bunch cilantro, leafy tops only

¼ cup Jalapeño Ponzu (page 12)

2 tablespoons seasoned rice wine vinegar

½ cup sesame oil

¼ cup cilantro leaves, for garnish

1 tablespoon black sesame seeds, for garnish

1   In a large stockpot over medium-high heat, bring water to a boil. Drop in the soba and cook for 6 to 8 minutes, stirring occasionally. Taste a noodle to make sure it is tender but firm to the bite. Transfer to a colander and run under cold water until the noodles have cooled down.

2   In a food processor, combine all the dressing ingredients except for the sesame oil. Blend for a few minutes, then whisk in the oil to emulsify the dressing. Transfer to a small bowl and set aside.

3   In a small mixing bowl combine the soy sauce, sesame oil, and mirin. Whisk well and set aside. Cut the tofu crosswise into 6 equal pieces, then cut each piece in half on the diagonal, making a triangle. Set aside.

4   Heat a large nonstick skillet over medium heat. Add the vegetable oil and then dip the tofu steaks into the soy mixture and place them in the skillet. Brown on each side for 3 to 4 minutes, seasoning with salt and white pepper. Transfer to a plate and set aside.

5   In a large mixing bowl, add the soba, half the vegetables, and half the dressing. Toss well, making sure to evenly distribute the vegetables. Transfer to a large serving platter and drizzle with more dressing if needed. Place the tofu steaks around the border of the noodles and then top with the remaining vegetables. Sprinkle with the cilantro leaves and black sesame seeds. Serve immediately.

Summer Buckwheat Noodles in Chilled Beef Broth

In the heat of the summer, one of the things we Koreans look forward to is having our traditional *mul naeng myun*. The chilled sweet beef broth paired with the chewy and nutty texture of the buckwheat noodles is such a treat. The Korean pear is bigger, crunchier, and not as sweet as the Japanese pear. When we lived in Arizona and it was 120 degrees, my mom would make this for us for lunch *and* dinner. Even to this day, I wait for the heat to strike and round up my friends to head to a noodle house in K-town for this refreshing delight. I encourage you to make this as a light supper at home with some grilled skewers on the side.

SERVES: 6
PREP TIME: 30 MINUTES
COOK TIME: 2 HOURS

1 pound beef brisket

8 ounces buckwheat noodles
(*naeng myun*), dried or frozen

3 tablespoons sesame oil

1 cup peeled and julienned Korean daikon

½ cup seasoned rice wine vinegar, plus more for serving

2 tablespoons granulated sugar

Salt and black pepper to taste

3 eggs, boiled and peeled

1 hot-house cucumber, julienned

1 Korean pear (*shingo*),
peeled and julienned

12 ice cubes

For Sweet Beef Broth
(makes 3 quarts):

3 quarts Bone-Marrow Stock,
chilled (page 148)

1 cup peeled and puréed Korean pear (*shingo*)

Salt and black pepper to taste

¼ cup chopped scallions, for garnish
Korean hot mustard, for serving

1 In a medium stockpot over high heat, place 2 quarts water and the beef brisket. Bring to a boil, then simmer over low heat until tender (about 1½ hours). The meat should not be fork tender like pulled pork; it should retain a little firmness. Transfer the meat to a plate to cool and set aside.

2 In a large stockpot, bring water to a boil. Add a pinch of salt, then add the noodles and cook for 6 to 8 minutes if using dried noodles and 4 to 5 minutes if frozen or fresh. Using tongs, stir occasionally to make sure the noodles do not clump together. When done, remove from the heat and immediately run the noodles under cold water, using the tongs to keep the noodles from clumping. Once the noodles are cool, let drain for a few minutes and then place in a mixing bowl, drizzle with sesame oil, and toss so that the noodles will keep their elasticity and do not clump. Set aside.

3 Make the Sweet Beef Broth: In a large mixing bowl blend the Bone Marrow Broth and puréed Korean pear together with a whisk. Season with salt and pepper and place in a pitcher or bowl and chill in the refrigerator until ready to use.

4 In a small mixing bowl, toss the daikon with the rice vinegar, sugar, and a pinch of salt. Set aside.

5 Slice the brisket into paper-thin slices going against the grain. Season with salt and black pepper.

6 Slice the boiled eggs in half. Set aside on a plate.

7 In 6 large deep soup bowls, evenly divide the noodles as if you are making a ball of the noodles. Top each mound of noodles with equal amounts of the daikon mixture, cucumber, pear, and brisket. Put 2 ice cubes on the bottom of each bowl and bring to the table.

8 At the table, pour the cold broth into each bowl. Top each bowl with one half boiled egg and garnish with the scallions.

9 Serve immediately, with the hot mustard and vinegar as condiments.

Simply Udon

Udon is another staple to have on hand for an afternoon snack or midnight meal, loved by kids and adults alike. Traditionally the Japanese add udon to a dashi broth and serve it with fish cakes. Here I share my own simple version, which is vegetarian. You can spice it up if you desire, but I like a clean broth to keep the purity of the dish. Serve this on a cold day for lunch or dinner.

SERVES: 4
PREP TIME: 20 MINUTES
COOK TIME: 20 MINUTES

2 quarts Veg Stock (page 12)

6 dried shiitake mushrooms, soaked in hot water, julienned

1 carrot, peeled and sliced

1 leek, white parts only, julienned

¼ Korean daikon, cut into ¼-inch-thick slices

2 packages (16 ounces) udon noodles

1 bunch spinach leaves

2 tablespoons soy sauce

Sea salt and white pepper to taste

½ package (8 ounces) extra-firm tofu, cut into 1-inch cubes

2 hard-boiled eggs, halved

1 In a large stockpot, bring the vegetable stock to a rolling boil. Add the mushrooms, carrots, leek, and daikon. Bring to a low simmer and cook for about 15 minutes.

2 Add the udon and boil for 2 to 3 minutes. Add the spinach and soy sauce. Season with sea salt and white pepper.

3 Drop the tofu in and cook for about 1 minute. Remove the soup from the heat.

4 In 4 large soup bowls, evenly divide the noodles, vegetables, tofu, and broth. Top each bowl with half of an egg. Serve immediately.

Sweet Potato Noodle Soup

Here's a recipe for *seolleongtang* or *sul lung tang*—what we know as bone-marrow soup. This cloudy milky concoction is a winter favorite. Best made a few days ahead, this soup is often served with some *ggakdugi*, aka icicle radish kimchee. My grandmother would add a little brisket for more flavor and protein, although traditionally the dish does not use beef. As a little meat never hurts, I stick with my grandmother's version.

SERVES: 4
PREP TIME: 2 HOURS
COOK TIME: 1½ HOURS

2 quarts Bone-Marrow Stock (page 148)

2 pounds oxtail bones

Sea salt and white pepper

4 ounces sweet potato noodles (*dang myun*, available in Asian markets), soaked in hot water for

about 30 minutes

1 pound beef brisket, boiled and shredded

¼ cup chopped scallions, for garnish

Steamed white rice

Icicle Radish Kimchee (page 38)

1 In a large stockpot bring the Bone-Marrow Stock and oxtail bones to a boil. Reduce the heat and simmer for about 1 hour. Season with salt and pepper to taste. Remove from the heat and strain well. Return the strained broth to the stockpot.

2 Bring the stock to a rolling boil and add the noodles. Boil for 4 to 5 minutes or until tender.

3 In 4 large soup bowls, evenly divide the noodles and broth. Top with the brisket and scallions. Serve with steamed white rice and Icicle Radish Kimchee.

Korean Noodle and Dumpling Soup

Gal guk su is another Korean favorite that we tend to crave during the wintertime. It is also a satisfying dish to snack on with a cocktail. Back in the day, tradition called for hand-torn noodles. My grandmother cheated though, and used udon noodles instead. To save time, you can buy prepared dumplings, but homemade dumplings really make this dish! So, the next time you're craving some Chinese wonton soup, try this delicious Korean alternative.

SERVES: 4
PREP TIME: 1 HOUR
COOK TIME: 15 MINUTES

2 quarts Bone-Marrow Stock (page 148)

¼ cup julienned leeks, white parts only

16 Modern Mandu, uncooked (page 88)

One 8-ounce package udon noodles

2 eggs, beaten

Sea salt and white pepper to taste

8 cloves garlic, thinly sliced and deep fried

4 sheets roasted seaweed (*nori*, available in Asian markets), for garnish

1 In a large stockpot, bring the stock to a rolling boil over medium-high heat. Add the leeks, reduce the heat to medium, and simmer for about 10 minutes.

2 Add the mandu and cook for 4 to 5 minutes. Add the udon noodles and cook for another 2 to 3 minutes.

3 Drop the beaten eggs in the pot while the broth is still boiling, swirling the eggs with chopsticks and breaking them up as they rise to the surface.

4 In 4 large soup bowls, evenly divide the noodles and dumplings, then pour the egg broth over all. Top with the fried garlic and crumble one sheet of roasted seaweed over each soup bowl. Serve immediately.

Chapter Five

It's All About the Rice!
From Pancakes to Rice Cakes

Sometimes I wonder what Koreans would do without rice. My grandfather never went a day in his entire life without eating at least one big mound of hot white rice. Even on Thanksgiving Day, my mom would have to cook rice for my gramps or he would not eat. I thought it was weird and asked my mom why he just didn't eat mashed potatoes like the rest of us. My mom said it's just not the same . . . and now that I am in my older years, I would have to agree. What's even better is exploring all the ways we can consume rice. From basic leek and rice flour pancakes to spicy stir-fried rice cakes (aka *tteokboki*) there is nothing better than a rice dish—especially when you had a lot to drink! The good news: Rice dishes are prominent on pub menus. My recipes can be enjoyed as a tasty quick snack or as a comforting main course.

I use Calrose rice in all of my recipes. Calrose is a white, medium grain, glutinous rice, used for sushi and in other Japanese cuisine. It is fluffier and lighter than a longer grained rice, like jasmine, which is used in Thai cuisine. See page 149 for instruction on cleaning and preparing rice for cooking.

Traditional Rice Pancakes (Pajeon)

My mother told me that when she was a little girl my grandfather would rush over to his local pub after work for some crispy *pajeon*. Sometimes he would bring home leftovers and my mom and her brother would fight over the little leek pancakes. The first time I had one at my grandmother's house, I fell in love. Before then all I knew of pancakes involved a lot of maple syrup and butter. Little did I know what I was missing out on! These traditional rice pancakes are perfect as an appetizer for a party or even served with some eggs and sausage for brunch. Whatever you pair with these little gems, make sure to make plenty. One is never enough.

SERVES: 4
PREP TIME: 10 MINUTES
COOK TIME: 15 MINUTES

1½ cups self-rising flour

½ teaspoon sea salt

1 teaspoon garlic powder

¼ teaspoon white pepper

1 clove garlic, mashed

1 egg

2 teaspoons soy sauce

1 tablespoon sesame oil

1½ cups ice-cold water (with cubes)

¼ cup sweet glutinous rice flour (*chapsal*)

2 leeks, white parts only, julienned

¼ cup vegetable oil

¼ cup chopped chives, for garnish

For Ginger-Soy Vinegar:

1 cup soy sauce

1 cup seasoned rice wine vinegar

¼ cup minced fresh ginger

1. In a large mixing bowl, combine the self-rising flour, sea salt, garlic powder, and white pepper. Add the mashed garlic clove, egg, soy sauce, and sesame oil and whisk well.

2. Add half of the water (without the ice cubes) and whisk well. Add the rice flour and remaining water (discarding the ice cubes) and whisk well. Fold in the leeks with a rubber spatula. Set batter aside.

3. In a medium mixing bowl, combine all of the ingredients together for the Ginger-Soy Vinegar. Transfer to a small serving bowl and set aside.

4. Heat a large nonstick skillet over medium heat. Add the vegetable oil and warm for 1 minute.

5. With a measuring cup, scoop ¼ cup of batter at a time and dollop in the pan, making sure to leave at least an inch all around so that the pancakes don't touch one another. Brown on each side for 3 to 4 minutes, or until cooked.

6. Transfer the pancakes to a serving platter and garnish with the chopped chives. Serve immediately with the Ginger-Soy Vinegar on the side.

Seafood Rice Pancakes (Haemul Pajeon)

What's even better than the leek pancake on the opposite page is this seafood one. I make it as a light supper or for brunch. Once perfected, this dish is pure culinary brilliance. The Pimento-Scallion Glaze adds a nice touch.

MAKES: 8 TO 10 PANCAKES
PREP TIME: 15 MINUTES
COOK TIME: 20 MINUTES

1½ cups self-rising flour

½ teaspoon sea salt

1 teaspoon garlic powder

¼ teaspoon white pepper

1 clove garlic, mashed

1 egg

2 teaspoons soy sauce

1 tablespoon sesame oil

1½ cups ice-cold water (with cubes)

¼ cup sweet glutinous rice flour (*chapsal*)

¼ pound rock shrimp, shelled and chopped

¼ pound lump crabmeat, flaked

½ cup chopped scallions

¼ cup vegetable oil, for frying

¼ cup chopped chives, for garnish

For Pimento-Scallion Glaze:

½ cup red chile bean paste (*gochujang*)

1 cup finely chopped scallions, white parts only

½ cup soy sauce

½ cup seasoned rice wine vinegar

¼ cup brown sugar

¼ cup coarse chile pepper flakes (*gochugaru*)

½ cup sesame oil

1   In a large mixing bowl combine the self-rising flour, sea salt, garlic powder, and white pepper. Add the mashed garlic clove, egg, soy sauce, and sesame oil and whisk well.

2   Add half of the water (without the ice cubes), and whisk well. Add the rice flour and remaining water and whisk well. Fold in the shrimp, crabmeat, and scallions with a rubber spatula. Set batter aside.

3   In a medium mixing bowl, combine all the ingredients for the Pimento-Scallion Glaze except the sesame oil. Once all the other ingredients are mixed well, whisk in the sesame oil. Transfer to a small serving bowl and set aside.

4   Heat a large nonstick skillet over medium heat. Add the vegetable oil and warm for 1 minute.

5   With a measuring cup, scoop ⅓ cup of batter at a time and dollop in the pan, making sure to leave at least an inch all around so that the pancakes don't touch one another. Brown on each side for 4 to 5 minutes, or until cooked.

6   Transfer to a serving platter and garnish with the chopped chives. Serve immediately with the Pimento-Scallion Glaze on the side.

Eggceptional Egg-Fried Rice

One of my all-time favorite basic snacks is Korean egg-fried rice. The toasted flavor from the sesame oil makes this so delicious. It's great for breakfast paired with some bacon or some hot dogs, or as a light snack with a bowl of your favorite kimchee. Just make sure to use cold leftover rice for best results.

SERVES: 4
PREP TIME: 5 MINUTES
COOK TIME: 10 MINUTES

2 tablespoons sesame oil

4 eggs, beaten

4 cups cooked Calrose rice, chilled

2 tablespoons soy sauce

1 teaspoon garlic powder

1 teaspoon sea salt

½ teaspoon white pepper

2 tablespoons chopped scallions, green parts only, for garnish

1 In a large skillet, preheat a wok over medium-high heat. Add the sesame oil and warm for 1 minute. Add the eggs and scramble quickly using the back of a wok ladle.

2 Add the rice and continue to cook for 3 to 4 minutes, constantly stirring with a wok ladle. Add the soy sauce and seasonings and give the rice mixture one more quick toss.

3 Transfer to 4 serving plates. Garnish with the scallions and serve immediately.

Kimchee Fried Rice

There are two things that I always want when I'm in a Korean pub: One is Korean fried chicken and the other is kimchee fried rice. It is the ultimate bar food and is great with a cold beer or a bottle of chilled *soju*. The spicy flavor of this quintessential fried rice melds perfectly with the sweetness of the twice-fried pork belly and the creamy texture of the fried egg yolk. It's the best thing to make with surplus rice and kimchee. If you don't have pork belly, I suggest using bacon, hot dogs, or even Spam.

SERVES: 4
PREP TIME: 15 MINUTES
COOK TIME: 20 MINUTES

¼ pound pork belly, skin off, cut lengthwise into ¼-inch slices

¼ cup soy sauce

¼ cup mirin

Sea salt and white pepper to taste

2 tablespoons sesame oil, for frying

1 In a medium mixing bowl, combine the pork belly, soy sauce, and mirin. Season with salt and white pepper. Set aside.

2 Heat a skillet over medium-high heat. Sear the pork belly for 3 to 4 minutes on each side until the marinade caramelizes on the meat. Set the skillet aside, letting the pork continue to cook off the heat for about 10 minutes. Slice crosswise into ¼-inch strips and transfer to a bowl.

3 Heat a wok or large nonstick skillet over medium-high heat. Add the sesame oil and warm for 1 minute. Add the reserved pork belly, kimchee, and Korean peppers and sauté for 3 to 4 minutes, stirring constantly.

2 cups kimchee, julienned

¼ cup Korean peppers (*gochu*), sliced into rings

4 cups cooked Calrose rice, chilled

¼ cup kimchee juice, poured from a kimchee jar

¼ cup chopped scallions

1 tablespoon vegetable oil

4 eggs

1 tablespoon roasted and salted sesame seeds, for garnish

4 Add the rice and break it up with the back of a wok ladle, tossing constantly to prevent it from sticking to the wok. Add the kimchee juice and scallions, and season with salt and white pepper. Remove from the heat and set aside.

5 Heat another nonstick skillet over medium-low heat. Add the vegetable oil and warm for 1 minute. Crack the eggs into the pan and cook sunny side up until done. Season with salt and white pepper.

6 Place a mound of fried rice on 4 separate plates and top each mound with a fried egg. Garnish with the sesame seeds and serve immediately.

Korean-Style Sushi (Kimbap)

Whether you're on a picnic or wanting a quick light snack at a bar, Korean-style sushi rolls do the trick. These rolls are perfect to serve at a sushi party and are just right for the novice sushi eater since there is no raw seafood involved. We primarily use seasoned ground beef, fish cakes, or kimchee, but have fun coming up with your own filling variations! You'll need a bamboo sushi roller, which you can find at most Asian markets.

SERVES: 8
PREP TIME: 30 MINUTES
COOK TIME: 1 HOUR

1 pound ground beef
Ginger-Soy Marinade (page 24)
4 cups cooked Calrose rice, hot
2 tablespoons seasoned rice wine vinegar
2 tablespoons mirin
1 teaspoons sugar
8 sheets roasted seaweed (*nori*, available in Asian markets)
1 bag spinach leaves, boiled and drained
1 cup julienned carrots
8 strips sweet daikon pickle (*takuan*, available in Asian markets)

For Egg Omelet Quiche:
4 eggs
¼ cup heavy cream
2 teaspoons granulated sugar
2 tablespoons mirin
½ teaspoon sea salt

Jalapeño Ponzu (page 12), for dipping

1 Preheat the oven to 325°F. Grease an 8 x 8-inch casserole pan.

2 In a medium mixing bowl, whisk together all the Egg Omelet Quiche ingredients. Pour the mixture into the prepared casserole and cover with aluminum foil. Bake in a water bath for 20 minutes. You can test for doneness by sticking the tip of a knife or chopstick in the middle of the quiche. When it comes out clean, it is ready. Let cool completely, and invert the quiche onto a plate.

3 In a medium saucepan, boil the ground beef in the marinade over medium-low heat, stirring to prevent sticking. Cook until well done, about 8 minutes. Remove from the heat and drain off the liquid and juices. Transfer the beef to a bowl and set aside.

4 In a large mixing bowl, combine the hot rice, rice vinegar, mirin, and sugar. Using a rice paddle, mix well. Let cool for 5 to 6 minutes.

5 Slice the egg omelet quiche into 8 long strips, about the same size as your daikon pickle strips. On a flat surface, place 1 sheet of seaweed, the smooth side facing up, on your bamboo sushi roller. Make sure the sheet is positioned with the long side facing you so that you get more length out of your sushi roll.

6 Spread one-eighth of the rice on the bottom half of the seaweed. Then add a row of beef across the rice, along with the spinach, carrots, egg strips, and pickled daikon. Using your sushi roller, pull the sushi toward you to tighten and then carefully roll up the sushi. Seal with a dab of warm water along the edge of the seaweed. Grip the roller for a few minutes to make sure you form a tight and even roll.

7 Repeat until you are finished with all 8 rolls. Cut each roll into 8 even pieces.

8 Arrange on a serving platter and serve with the Jalapeño Ponzu on the side.

Spicy Stir-Fried Rice Cakes (Tteokboki)

This is probably one of the most popular dishes at a Korean pub or café. The spicy sweet flavor of the sauce drenches the chewy goodness of the rice cake cylinders, or *tteok*, which is similar to a rice gnocchi, although a little denser and more glutinous in texture. You can make this dish heartier with pork butt or bacon—I've even topped these rice cakes with beef Bolognese. Here I add a bit of crunch with vegetables and some fish cakes.

SERVES: 4
PREP TIME: 10 MINUTES
COOK TIME: 30 MINUTES

2 tablespoons vegetable oil

½ yellow onion, sliced into ½-inch strips

1 carrot, peeled and sliced on a diagonal, into ¼-inch-thick rounds

½ head Napa cabbage, sliced into ½-inch strips

Sea salt and white pepper to taste

½ package Korean rice cake cylinders, cut in half

1 package fish cakes, sliced into ½-inch strips (available in Asian markets)

1 bunch scallions, white parts only, sliced into 2-inch stalks

1 tablespoon granulated sugar

1 tablespoon black sesame seeds, for garnish

1 tablespoon roasted and salted sesame seeds, for garnish

For Spicy Chile Slurry:

½ cup red bean chile paste (*gochujang*)

1 cup kimchee juice

¼ cup mirin

½ cup water

2 tablespoons finely ground chile powder (*gochugaru*)

3 tablespoons cornstarch slurry (1 part cornstarch and 2 parts cold water)

1 In a medium saucepan, combine all the ingredients for the Spicy Chile Slurry except for the cornstarch slurry. Bring to a low boil over medium heat, then simmer for 10 to 15 minutes.

2 Whisk in the cornstarch slurry. Cook over low heat for 2 to 3 minutes or until the mixture has started to thicken. Remove from the heat and set aside.

3 Heat a wok or large nonstick skillet over medium-high heat. Add the vegetable oil and warm for 1 minute.

4 Add the yellow onion and carrots and sauté for 2 to 3 minutes. Add the Napa cabbage, and season with salt and white pepper. Add half of the slurry and toss to coat the vegetables. Lower the heat to medium-low.

5 Add the rice cakes and cook for 2 to 3 minutes, stirring constantly so that they don't stick to the pan. Add the remaining slurry if needed, so the rice cakes don't dry out, then add the fish cakes and scallions. Sprinkle with the sugar and toss again.

6 Cook for a few more minutes to let the sauce reduce and thicken a little.

7 Remove from the heat and divide equally between 4 serving plates. Garnish with both kinds of sesame seeds and serve immediately.

Royal Rice Cakes

For those not inclined to go the really spicy route, here is a more mild version of a Korean pub favorite. The sweet flavor of the Daikon-Soy Stir-Fry Sauce pairs beautifully with the rice cakes. I love to serve this as a first course when I'm having friends over for dinner, but if you throw in some julienned steak, you'll have a pasta main course—"Seoul style"—for the whole family. Even the kids will love it!

SERVES: 4
PREP TIME: 30 MINUTES
COOK TIME: 20 MINUTES

2 tablespoons vegetable oil

1 carrot, peeled and sliced on a diagonal, into ¼-inch-thick rounds

½ red onion, sliced into ½-inch strips

8 shiitake mushrooms, soaked in hot water, drained, and julienned

½ package Korean rice cake cylinders, cut in half

½ head Napa cabbage, sliced into ½-inch strips

1 bunch scallions, white parts only, sliced into 2-inch stalks

1 tablespoon granulated sugar

Sea salt and white pepper to taste

1 tablespoon black sesame seeds, for garnish

1 tablespoon roasted and salted sesame seeds, for garnish

For Daikon-Soy Stir-Fry Sauce:

1 cup Veg Stock (page 146)

½ cup soy sauce

¼ cup mirin

1 small Korean daikon, peeled and roasted

Sea salt and white pepper to taste

1. First, make the Daikon-Soy Stir-Fry Sauce: In a medium saucepan combine the vegetable stock, soy sauce, and mirin. Bring to a low boil over medium heat and simmer for 5 minutes.

2. Puree the roasted daikon in a food processor until it becomes a paste. Transfer to the sauce mixture in the saucepan and whisk well. Simmer for another 5 minutes. Season with salt and white pepper and set aside.

3. Heat a wok or large nonstick skillet over medium-high heat. Add the vegetable oil and warm for 1 minute.

4. Add the carrots and red onions and saute for 3 to 4 minutes. Add the mushrooms and cook for another 2 to 3 minutes. Add one half of the stir-fry sauce to the pan and reduce the heat to medium. Add the rice cakes and cook for another 3 to 4 minutes, stirring constantly so that they don't stick to the pan.

5. Add the Napa cabbage and scallions. Toss and cook for another 2 minutes. Sprinkle with the sugar and toss one more time. Season with salt and white pepper if needed.

6. Divide equally among 4 pasta bowls and sprinkle with both kinds of sesame seeds. Serve immediately.

The Korean Nacho — A Modernized Classic

One day my staff was begging me to make a Korean-Latin dish, but no matter how much they beg, I will never make a taco or burrito! However, I had tasted a new version of *tteokboki* at one of my favorite Korean pubs that featured melted cheese on top of a spicy rice cake. I was not a fan but I decided to play around with the concept and, low and behold, I created the infamous "Korean Nacho." What started out as a staff meal has turned into the number 2 seller off my Korean food truck. The crispiness of the rice cakes melds with the sweetness of the pork and the smokiness of the cheese sauce. Add some Kimchee Salsa and fried Korean peppers . . . and, well, you simply have a masterpiece!

SERVES: 4
PREP TIME: 30 MINUTES
COOK TIME: 1½ HOURS

1 pound pork butt

2 cups Ginger-Soy Marinade (see page 24)

1 can (12 ounces) Coke or other cola

For Chile-Cheese Queso (makes 3 cups; need 2 cups):

8 tablespoons unsalted butter

1 yellow onion, minced

2 tablespoons minced garlic

8 ounces Cheddar, grated

8 ounces Monterey Jack cheese, grated

1 cup heavy cream

4 ounces cream cheese

1 cup whole milk

1 teaspoon garlic powder

1 teaspoon onion powder

1 teaspoon finely ground chile powder (*gochugaru*)

1 teaspoon smoked paprika

1 teaspoon sea salt

½ teaspoon white pepper

2 tablespoons all-purpose flour

For Kimchee Salsa:

½ cup finely diced kimchee

¼ cup finely diced hot-house cucumber

¼ cup finely diced Korean daikon

½ red onion, finely diced

½ jalapeño pepper, seeds removed, finely diced

Juice of 1 lemon

1 tablespoon seasoned rice wine vinegar

Salt and white pepper to taste

Vegetable oil, for frying

½ package Korean rice cake cylinders, cut in half

8 Smoky Fried Peppers (page 135), skinned and sliced into diagonal rings, for garnish

¼ cup chopped scallions, green parts only, for garnish

1 tablespoon black sesame seeds, for garnish

1 tablespoon roasted and salted sesame seeds, for garnish

1 Preheat the oven to 325°F.

2 In a deep casserole dish, combine the pork butt, Ginger-Soy Marinade, and cola. Cover loosely with aluminum foil and bake for an hour and a half or until fork-tender. Remove from the oven and let cool. While still warm, pull apart with 2 forks and set meat aside in a bowl.

3 Meanwhile, make the Chile-Cheese Queso: Heat a medium saucepan over medium-low heat. Melt half the butter, being careful not to let it burn. Add the onion and garlic and cook for 3 to 4 minutes. Add the Cheddar and Monterey Jack, reduce the heat to low, and stir until the cheese starts to melt. Stir in the heavy cream then let the cheese melt completely.

4 Add the cream cheese to the saucepan, and when melted, add the whole milk and seasonings. Let simmer over low heat for 10 minutes, stirring occasionally.

5 Meanwhile, in a small saucepan, melt the remaining butter over low heat. Once it starts to bubble, stir in the flour and whisk until well incorporated. Let the mixture thicken for a few minutes before adding it to the cheese sauce. Whisk and cook for another 2 to 3 minutes. Taste and season with salt and pepper if necessary. Remove from the heat and set aside.

6 In a medium mixing bowl, combine all ingredients for the Kimchee Salsa, seasoning with salt and pepper before setting aside.

7 In a deep pan for frying, pour in 4 inches of vegetable oil and heat until it reaches 375°F when measured with a candy thermometer. Add the rice cakes and fry for 2 to 3 minutes. Remove immediately from the heat and distribute among 4 pasta bowls. Dollop each serving with ¼ cup Chile-Cheese Queso, add some pulled pork, and top with Kimchee Salsa. Place two Smoky Fried Peppers in each bowl, garnish with the scallions and both kinds of sesame seeds, and serve immediately.

Chapter Six

A Tribute to Pork: The Belly Itself

There is something so magical about pork—I don't know what I would do without it. As in most Asian diets, pork is a common protein in Korean cooking that we use to flavor and enhance soups, stews, and even our favorite vegetable dishes. Koreans have a special affinity for the belly, pork butt, shoulder, and neck meat. Our ancestors believed these are the best parts of the pig and yield the most flavor.

My grandfather ate pork belly, basically an uncured bacon, every day, as he claimed it prevented lung disease. I just think that was a convenient excuse, but I don't really blame gramps for that one.

Pork belly is delicious. We do everything from braising the belly to grilling, steaming, and even frying it. I include all methods in this chapter.

When visiting a Korean pub, you will always find at least five dishes that use pork belly and various other cuts of pork as well. I've dedicated my tribute to the pig to its belly, although a few co-stars from different parts of my favorite animal make an appearance in this chapter as well.

Grilled Pork Belly with Soy-Mirin Glaze

I frequent a local BBQ house that specializes in pork belly, and it's a must when ordering. Probably one of my favorite ways to eat pork belly is with a simple marinade grilled over the BBQ. I love it when the sugar caramelizes on the pork on the grill and the meat almost gets a burnt essence. The key is to cook it to the point of crispiness, but there should still be a pull when chewing. That's when you know it's ready to eat. I use this recipe to make my spin on a BLT for my truck. It's quite addictive, as you will soon see.

SERVES: 4
PREP TIME: 10 MINUTES
COOK TIME: 30 MINUTES

1 pound pork belly, skin removed, sliced lengthwise into ¼-inch-thick pieces

1 cup soy sauce

1 cup mirin

Sea salt and white pepper to taste

Vegetable oil or pork fat, for seasoning the grill

2 tablespoons chopped scallions, for garnish

1 tablespoon roasted and salted sesame seeds, for garnish

For Soy-Mirin Glaze:

1 cup Bone-Marrow Stock (page 148)

½ cup soy sauce

½ cup mirin

1 teaspoon onion powder

¼ cup honey

3 tablespoons cornstarch slurry (1 part cornstarch and 2 parts cold water)

1   In a large mixing bowl, combine the pork belly, soy sauce, and mirin. Toss well and season with salt and white pepper. Cover with plastic wrap and let marinate in the refrigerator for 30 minutes, preferably overnight.

2   Meanwhile, make the Soy-Mirin Glaze: Combine all the ingredients except for the cornstarch slurry in a medium saucepan and bring to a low boil over medium heat. Simmer for 10 to 15 minutes, or until the sauce reduces by half.

3   Gradually whisk the cornstarch slurry into the glaze and cook for 2 to 3 minutes, until the sauce slightly thickens. Remove from the heat and set aside.

4   Remove the pork belly from the refrigerator and let stand for about 5 minutes at room temperature. Heat a grill or grill pan over medium-high heat and brush it well with the vegetable oil or pork fat.

5   Place the pork-belly slices on the grill and cook for 3 to 4 minutes on each side. Repeat twice, for a total cook time of 18 to 24 minutes, constantly flipping so the belly doesn't stick to the grill. When done, the meat will start to caramelize and you will see a crispy border on the ends. Transfer to a serving platter and let rest for a few minutes.

6   Drizzle some of the Soy-Mirin Glaze on top of the pork belly. Garnish with the scallions and sesame seeds. Use any remaining sauce for dipping. Serve immediately.

Spicy BBQ Pork

Daeji bulgogi, aka spicy BBQ pork, is always a crowd favorite at the pub. It has a real kick to it but a bowl of rice will cool your palate. I love making this during the summer for house parties and turning it into a lettuce wrap bar. I have also been known to top my version of a pork burger with it. The sweet and spicy marinade really takes any sandwich to the next level. Keep in mind that you can always pare down the amount of spice on this rub if it is too hot for your taste buds. Marinating the pork overnight is best, as this will yield the most flavor when you cook it.

SERVES: 4
PREP TIME: 10 MINUTES
COOK TIME: 45 MINUTES

1 pound pork roast, sliced into deli-thin slices

½ cup Smoky Chile Rub (page 22)

1 can beer

Sea salt and white pepper to taste

Vegetable oil or pork fat, for seasoning the grill

1 white onion, sliced into ¼-inch-thick rings

1 tablespoon roasted and salted sesame seeds, for garnish

1 In a large mixing bowl, combine the pork roast, Smoky Chile Rub, and beer. Mix well with your hands to make sure the marinade is distributed evenly. Season with salt and white pepper. Cover the bowl with plastic wrap and refrigerate for at least 30 minutes but preferably overnight.

2 Remove the pork from the refrigerator and let stand at room temperature for at least 10 minutes.

3 Heat a grill or grill pan over medium-high heat and brush with the vegetable oil or pork fat. Place the onion rings on the grill and cook for 2 to 3 minutes on each side. Season with salt and white pepper. Transfer to a serving platter and set aside.

4 Place the pork on the grill and cook for 4 to 5 minutes on each side, or until cooked through. Transfer to the serving platter with the grilled onions and garnish with the sesame seeds. Serve immediately.

Hangover Stew

One of the best things about going to a Korean pub is that you can eat a remedy stew or soup *while* you drink to prevent a hangover from occurring the next morning. *Gamjatang* (aka pork and potato stew) is a smart pick when you know you will be going through several bottles at one sitting. I also like to order *gamjatang* "to go" for the morning after, just in case. We Koreans believe that the hot peppers and loads of spice will sweat out all the toxins in your body. Whether true or not, this is the kind of dish that is always better the second day around. So, be sure to make enough for leftovers, whether you're drinking or not.

SERVES: 4, PLUS LEFTOVERS
PREP TIME: 20 MINUTES
COOK TIME: 1½ HOURS

2 pounds pork butt, cut into
3 x 3-inch pieces
2 cups Smoky Chile Rub (page 22)
2 yellow onions, sliced ¼ inch thick
¼ cup thinly sliced garlic cloves
2 quarts Pork Stock (page 148)
2 cans beer
¼ cup soy sauce
1 tablespoon garlic powder
1 tablespoon onion powder
2 tablespoons coarse chile pepper
flakes (*gochugaru*)
3 tablespoons sugar
2 tablespoons sesame oil
1 pound new potatoes, washed
and cut in half lengthwise
12 Korean peppers (*gochu*)
Sea salt and white pepper to taste
¼ cup chopped scallions, for
garnish

1 In a large mixing bowl, combine the pork butt and Smoky Chile Rub. Mix well and cover with plastic wrap. Refrigerate for at least 30 minutes.

2 Heat a large stockpot over medium-high heat. Add the onions and garlic, and sauté for 2 to 3 minutes. Add the marinated pork butt and sear the meat on both sides for 3 to 4 minutes, or until nicely golden brown. Add the stock and beer. Bring to a boil for 5 minutes.

3 Reduce the heat to medium-low and add the soy sauce, garlic and onion powders, chile pepper flakes, sugar, and sesame oil. Cover and simmer for about 30 minutes.

4 Add the potatoes and cook for another 20 minutes.

5 Add the Korean peppers and season with salt and white pepper. Cook for another 10 minutes.

6 Divide the soup among 4 large pasta bowls: Make sure to place 2 pieces of pork, 3 to 4 pieces of potato, and 2 to 3 peppers in each bowl. Add some onions and broth to each bowl and garnish with the scallions. Serve immediately.

Bossam-Style Steamed Pork Belly

My first memory of pork belly was watching my grandfather eat it *bossam* style, which is our version of pork belly wrapped in Napa cabbage. At the time I was pretty young and was not keen on the dish. Perhaps my palate was not mature enough to appreciate the clean flavors of the pork and the spicy accents from the daikon and a smear of *ssamjang*, which is a traditional Korean lettuce-wrap paste. Little did I know what I was missing! Now, at least once a month, I order pork belly bossam at a particular Korean pub in L.A. I enjoy it with a glass of Chardonnay, as the sweet vanilla undertones of the wine complement this dish.

SERVES: 6 TO 8
PREP TIME: 30 MINUTES
COOK TIME: 1½ HOURS

4 cloves garlic

1 two-inch piece fresh ginger, peeled

1 yellow onion, peeled and cut in half

1 teaspoon whole black peppercorns

1 tablespoon sea salt

2 quarts Pork Stock (page 148)

2 pounds whole pork belly, skin removed

For Bossam:

1 head Napa cabbage, cleaned and cut in quarters lengthwise

¼ cup sea salt

½ cup thinly sliced garlic cloves, for garnish

For Spicy Pickled Daikon:

1 Korean daikon, peeled and julienned

2 tablespoons sea salt

¼ cup seasoned rice wine vinegar

2 tablespoons sugar

2 tablespoons minced garlic cloves

1 tablespoon finely ground chile powder (*gochugaru*)

3 tablespoons sesame oil

For *Ssamjang*:

½ cup red bean chile paste (*gochujang*)

½ cup Korean miso paste (*doengjang*)

¼ cup soy sauce

¼ cup seasoned rice wine vinegar

3 tablespoons granulated sugar

1 jalapeño pepper, seeds removed

¼ cup sesame oil

1 In a large stockpot over medium-high heat, combine the garlic, ginger, onion, peppercorns, salt, and pork stock and bring to a boil. Add the pork belly and boil for about 5 minutes, then reduce the heat medium-low. Cover and simmer for 1 to 1½ hours. The pork belly should be tender but firm.

2 Meanwhile, make the Spicy Pickled Daikon: Place the daikon in a medium mixing bowl. Sprinkle with half of the sea salt and toss well. Let sit for about 10 minutes to allow the radish to start to pickle. Rinse with cold water and drain well. Sprinkle with the remaining salt and repeat the sitting, rinsing, and draining process. Transfer to a clean mixing bowl and add all the other ingredients. Mix well, cover with plastic wrap, and refrigerate until serving.

3 Next, prepare the *Bossam*: Take each quarter of the Napa cabbage and sprinkle, layer by layer, with half of the sea salt. Let sit to allow the cabbage to soften. Rinse well under cold water, making sure to remove excess salt from the layers. Repeat the steps again, then let drain in a colander.

4 Finally, prepare the *Ssamjang*: In a food processor, combine all the ingredients and purée until smooth. Transfer to a small condiment dish, cover with plastic wrap, and refrigerate until serving.

5 Remove the cooked pork belly from the pot and let cool for about 15 minutes. On a cutting board, cut the pork across in 3 pieces, then cut each piece into ¼-inch-thick slices.

6 Transfer the sliced pork belly to the middle of a serving platter and surround with the Napa cabbage quarters and sliced garlic. Serve immediately, with the Spicy Pickled Daikon and *Ssamjang* on the side.

Egg-Battered Pork Belly

It is very common for Koreans to eat fish, meat, and vegetables in what we refer to as *jeon*, basically anything dredged in flour and then dipped in a pure egg batter. It's a simple way to turn a plain piece of meat or vegetables into something magical. You can always find various *jeon* items at a pub or serve them as appetizers at a dinner party. *Jeon*-style pork belly is one of my favorites. It's like having breakfast in a great little package any time of day. Consider serving it for brunch along with some potatoes.

SERVES: 4
PREP TIME: 10 MINUTES
COOK TIME: 10 MINUTES

1 pound pork belly, skin removed, cut into 2-inch pieces, about ¼ inch thick

Sea salt and white pepper to taste

1 cup all-purpose flour

3 eggs, beaten

2 tablespoons vegetable oil

½ cup Ginger-Soy Vinegar (page 56)

2 tablespoons chopped scallions, for garnish

1 Lay the pork belly pieces flat on a sheet pan. Season with salt and white pepper on both sides. Place the all-purpose flour and beaten eggs in two separate bowls.

2 Heat a large nonstick skillet over medium-high heat. Add the vegetable oil and warm for 1 minute. Reduce the heat to medium.

3 Dredge the pork belly in the flour and then dip in egg. Place in the skillet and cook on each side for 4 to 5 minutes, or cooked through.

4 Transfer to a serving platter and garnish with the scallions. Serve immediately, with the Ginger-Soy Vinegar on the side for dipping.

Spam and Eggs

I love going to any Korean market and seeing the rows of Spam on display on the top shelves. It saddens me when people think of it as mystery meat. Spam is actually seasoned ham with water and spices, all blended together. It's magical meat, and I could eat this salty canned ham every day. My little nephew loves Sundays because it's "Spam Sunday" and he looks forward to my sister-in-law frying it up with some scrambled eggs, white rice, and kimchee. Little does Junior know that his Sunday brunch ritual was conceived at a pub. I'm sure he will really appreciate it when he's all grown up. I know I do!

SERVES: 4
PREP TIME: 5 MINUTES
COOK TIME: 20 MINUTES

2 tablespoons vegetable oil
8 eggs
Sea salt and black pepper to taste
1 can Spam, sliced into ¼-inch pieces (about 8 slices)
4 cups cooked white Calrose rice, hot
2 tablespoons roasted and salted sesame seeds, for garnish

For Chile Maple Syrup
(makes about ½ cup):
½ cup pure maple syrup
2 teaspoons finely ground chile powder (*gochugaru*)
½ teaspoon cinnamon
1 teaspoon smoked paprika

1 First, make the Chile Maple Syrup: In a small saucepan over medium heat, combine the maple syrup, chile powder, cinnamon, and smoked paprika. Bring to a low simmer and cook for about 10 minutes to allow the flavors to meld. Remove from the heat and cover the pot with aluminum foil to keep warm.

2 Heat a large nonstick skillet over medium-low heat. Add the vegetable oil and warm for 1 minute. Crack all 8 eggs into the skillet and cook sunny-side up for 3 to 4 minutes. Season with salt and pepper.

3 Heat another large nonstick skillet over medium-high heat. Add the Spam slices and brown on each side for 2 to 3 minutes, or until they attain a nice crust. Remove from the heat.

4 To assemble, place 1 cup of the hot rice on the middle of a serving plate. Top with 2 fried eggs and 2 slices of Spam. Drizzle with the Chile Maple Syrup, sprinkle with the sesame seeds, and serve immediately.

Stir-Fried Pork Belly with Kimchee

For those that choose to pass on the carbs but love the flavor of *tteokboki* (aka Spicy Stir-Fried Rice Cakes), you're in luck with this protein-packed dish. A lot of my Angeleno friends love this dish since they are always watching their waistlines. Of course, I prefer to put this on a bed of hot white rice, but the choice is yours. The kimchee juice called for can simply be poured from any kimchee jar you have on hand.

SERVES: 4, PLUS LEFTOVERS
PREP TIME: 15 MINUTES
COOK TIME: 15 MINUTES

2 tablespoons vegetable oil

½ pound pork belly, skin removed, cut into 1-inch pieces, about ¼ inch thick

1 cup Classic Napa Kimchee (page 34), julienned

1 carrot, julienned

4 Korean peppers (*gochu*), cut in diagonal rings

¼ cup kimchee juice, poured from a kimchee jar

1 tablespoon red chile bean paste (*gochujang*)

1 tablespoon soy sauce

1 bunch scallions, white parts only, julienned

1 tablespoon sugar

Sea salt and white pepper to taste

2 tablespoons chopped scallions, green parts only, for garnish

1 Heat a large nonstick skillet over medium-high heat. Add the vegetable oil and warm for 1 minute. Add the pork belly and brown for 2 to 3 minutes. Then add the kimchee and carrot. Sauté, stirring, for another 2 to 3 minutes.

2 Add the Korean peppers, kimchee juice, red chile bean paste, and soy sauce. Mix well and cook for another 2 to 3 minutes. Add the scallions and sugar and toss again. Season with salt and white pepper.

3 Transfer to a large pasta bowl, sprinkle with the scallions, and serve immediately.

Chapter Seven

A Round Table of Ground: Meatballs to Meatloaf

Whoever invented the concept of ground meat is a genius! Aside from the glorious burger that we all know and love, ground meat is used in so many different applications on the Korean menu. Especially in a pub, there is a plethora of ground meat–based options: All will give you that true comfort food feel. Whether used in a fried-rice dish, like Om Rice, or in Mama Lee's (that's my grams) version of meatloaf, you can always count on seeing some good old ground in the house, and in this chapter!

When using ground beef, I prefer ground rib-eye as it has the most marbling, and therefore, the fattiest and most delicious taste. If your local supermarket doesn't carry ground rib-eye, you can always as the butcher at the meat counter to grind up some scraps for you.

Chicken Meatballs with a Magnolia Berry Glaze

I don't know any cuisine that does not have some version of a meatball. In fact, it is the one item I always look for on the menu when dining out at ethnic restaurants. I love learning about new flavor profiles as I savor the juiciness of the ground meat. Not to mention, meatballs make amazing appetizers. My take on the Korean meatball incorporates the fruity and floral flavors of the magnolia berry tree, which grows in Korea. During the harvest, Koreans have *omija*, a magnolia tea, at the end of the meal. The first time I tried the drink I thought what a nice sauce it would make for chicken or fish. Leftover Magnolia Berry Glaze can be refrigerated for 2 weeks and used on grilled fish or a nice thick pork chop.

SERVES: 6
PREP TIME: 5 MINUTES
COOK TIME: 45 MINUTES

1 pound ground chicken
1 small yellow onion, puréed in a food processor
1 egg
1 tablespoon soy sauce
1 tablespoon sesame oil
1 teaspoon garlic powder
1 teaspoon onion powder
1 teaspoon sea salt

½ teaspoon white pepper
2 cups panko breadcrumbs
Vegetable oil, for deep frying

For the Magnolia Berry Glaze:
1 quart Chicken Stock (page 147)
1 cup magnolia berry syrup (available in Korean markets or online)
¼ cup soy sauce
¼ cup seasoned rice wine vinegar
½ cup mirin

2 teaspoon garlic powder
2 teaspoon onion powder
1 teaspoon finely ground chile powder (*gochugaru*)
1 teaspoon smoked paprika

1 bunch chives, chopped, for garnish
1 tablespoon black sesame seeds, for garnish
1 tablespoon roasted and salted sesame seeds, for garnish

1 In a large mixing bowl, combine all the meatball ingredients except the breadcrumbs and vegetable oil. Mix to incorporate well. Add the breadcrumbs a little at a time. If the mixture seems too wet, add a little more breadcrumbs to bind it. Place in the refrigerator to chill for about 15 minutes.

2 Meanwhile, in a medium saucepan over medium heat, combine all the ingredients for the Magnolia Berry Glaze. Bring to a low boil and simmer for 15 to 20 minutes, stirring occasionally, or until the sauce has reduced by a third. Remove from the heat and set aside.

3 Preheat the oven to 400°F. Remove the meatball mixture from the fridge and form 18 meatballs. Arrange on a sheet pan and place in the freezer to chill for 10 to 15 minutes.

4 In a large stockpot, pour in 2 tablespoons of vegetable oil and heat over medium-high heat until it reaches 375°F when measured with a candy or deep-fry thermometer. Remove the meatballs from the freezer and deep-fry until golden brown, about 3 to 4 minutes.

5 Using a slotted spoon, transfer the meatballs to a large mixing bowl and add the glaze. Toss well and arrange the meatballs on a baking pan. Bake for 8 to 10 minutes, or until the ground chicken is cooked through.

6 Transfer to a serving platter, garnish with the chives and both kinds of sesame seeds, and serve hot.

Mama Lee's Meatloaf

Known in the Korean and Japanese pubs as "hamburger steak," this Korean take on meatloaf is as comforting as the American favorite. Traditionally made from a combination of ground beef with onions, egg, and panko, it literally melts in your mouth; I always look forward to sopping up all the brown soy gravy that it is covered in. I up the ante by substituting ground rib-eye steak for the ground beef: the marbled texture of the steak takes it to another level. Serve it on a bed of hot rice or mashed potatoes.

SERVES: 6 TO 8
PREP TIME: 15 MINUTES
COOK TIME: 1 HOUR

1 pound ground rib-eye, Kobe or Angus steak

1 small yellow onion, puréed in a food processor

1 egg

1 tablespoon soy sauce

1 tablespoon sesame oil

1 teaspoon garlic powder

1 teaspoon onion powder

1 teaspoon sea salt

½ teaspoon black pepper

2 cups panko breadcrumbs

2 tablespoons vegetable oil, for frying

For Soy-Onion Demi:

1 quart Bone-Marrow Stock (page 148)

1 large yellow onion, puréed in a food processor

1 cup soy sauce

1 cup mirin

½ cup brown sugar

½ cup Shiitake Chicharones (page 134)

1 bunch chives, chopped, for garnish

2 tablespoons roasted and salted sesame seeds, for garnish

1 In a large mixing bowl, combine the ground steak, onion, egg, soy sauce, sesame oil, and the spices. Mix to incorporate well. Add the breadcrumbs a little at a time. If the mixture seems too wet, add a little more breadcrumbs to bind it. Place in the refrigerator to chill for about 30 minutes.

2 Meanwhile, in a medium saucepan over medium-high heat, combine all the ingredients for the Soy-Onion Demi. Bring to a low boil and simmer for 25 to 30 minutes, or until the sauce has reduced by half. Remove from the heat and set aside.

3 Preheat the oven to 400°F. Remove the meatloaf mixture from the fridge and form 8 patties about 1 inch thick. Place on a sheet pan and chill in the freezer for 10 to 15 minutes so they set.

4 Heat a large nonstick skillet over medium-high heat. Add the vegetable oil and warm for 1 minute. Remove the meatloaf patties from the freezer and sear on both sides for 3 to 4 minutes, or until a nice brown crust has been attained.

5 Transfer to a baking sheet and bake for 6 to 8 minutes, or until medium-well.

6 Transfer to a serving platter and top each patty with 2 tablespoons of Soy-Onion Demi. Top with the Shiitake Chicharones. Garnish with the chives and sesame seeds and serve immediately.

Curry Burger Rice

Normally this dish is prepared in a stone pot so the rice on the bottom will crust—as in *bibimbap*, our country's best-known rice bowl. The sizzling sound that is made when the server brings out this dish is amazing. This simple recipe is a great alternative to "burger night." Feel free to substitute ground turkey, chicken, or pork for the beef. As a bonus, you can serve any leftover vegetable curry over a bed of pasta the next day.

SERVES: 4
PREP TIME: 15 MINUTES
COOK TIME: 1 HOUR

1 pound ground beef

Sea salt and black pepper to taste

2 tablespoons vegetable oil

4 cups cooked Calrose rice, hot

2 tablespoons chopped scallions, for garnish

For the Curry:

2 tablespoons sesame oil

1 large yellow onion, cut into large dice

1 cup baby carrots

2 russet potatoes, peeled and cut into 1-inch cubes

1 quart Veg Stock (page 146)

Sea salt and white pepper to taste

1 box Japanese or Korean curry blocks (available in Asian markets)

1 cup Greek yogurt

1 cup frozen peas

1 First, make the curry: Heat a large stockpot over medium-high heat. Add the sesame oil and warm for 1 minute. Add the onion and brown for a few minutes. Add the carrots and potatoes and sauté for another 4 to 5 minutes. Add the stock and season with salt and white pepper. Bring to a boil and then reduce the heat to medium-low. Cover and simmer for 20 to 30 minutes, until the potatoes are fork-tender.

2 Form the ground beef into 4 patties about 1 inch thick. Season on both sides with salt and pepper.

3 Heat a large nonstick skillet over medium-high heat. Add the vegetable oil and warm for 1 minute. Pan-fry the beef patties on each side for 4 to 5 minutes, or until you have reached your desired doneness for the beef. Remove from the heat and set aside.

4 Add the curry blocks to the stockpot and stir, making sure the curry has dissolved evenly. Add the yogurt and peas and stir. Cover and cook for another 3 to 4 minutes.

5 Place 1 cup of rice on each of 4 dinner plates. Place 1 beef patty on top of the rice. Top the beef with ½ cup curry, garnish with the scallions, and serve immediately.

Om Rice

This hearty rice dish is not just a treat at your local Korean pub. It was also a dinner that my mom made from leftovers when she did not have time to run out and get groceries. Think of a fluffy egg omelet crêpe filled with tasty ground beef fried rice. It's absolutely divine. And you can't forget the ketchup—it completes this dish. Try serving this for brunch or enjoy as a midnight snack.

SERVES: 4
PREP TIME: 15 MINUTES
COOK TIME: 40 MINUTES

2 tablespoons sesame oil

1 small white onion, diced

½ pound ground beef

1 large carrot, diced

½ cup frozen peas

6 cups cooked Calrose rice, chilled overnight

1 teaspoon garlic powder

1 teaspoon onion powder

Sea salt and white pepper to taste

2 tablespoons soy sauce

¼ cup chopped scallions, for garnish

For Egg Omelet:

10 eggs

¼ cup heavy cream

2 tablespoons mirin

4 tablespoons self-rising flour

1 tablespoon sugar

Sea salt and white pepper to taste

4 tablespoons vegetable oil

Chile Ketchup:

1 cup tomato ketchup

2 tablespoons red chile bean paste (*gochujang*)

1 First, make the Chile Ketcup: In a small mixing bowl, combine the ketchup and red chile bean paste and mix well with a fork or small whisk. Set aside.

2 In a large mixing bowl, whisk together all the ingredients for the egg omelet except the vegetable oil.

3 Heat a 10-inch nonstick skillet heat over medium heat. Add 1 tablespoon vegetable oil and warm for 1 minute. Add one-fourth of the egg batter and swirl it around like you are making a crêpe. Lower the heat to medium-low and, with a rubber spatula, lift the edges so that you can flip it over once it's cooked. Cook the other side for 1 minute. Transfer to a sheet pan and repeat 3 more times with the rest of the batter and vegetable oil. Set aside.

4 Heat a large wok over medium-high heat. Add the sesame oil and warm for 1 minute. Add the onion and sauté for 1 to 2 minutes. Add the ground beef and brown for 3 to 4 minutes. Add the carrots and sauté for another 2 to 3 minutes. Add the peas and rice. Toss with the back of a wok ladle, making sure the rice does not stick to the pan. Add all of the seasonings and the soy sauce. Continue to stir and toss until the rice is done. Remove from the heat.

5 Place 1 egg crêpe on each of 4 dinner plates. Add one-fourth of the fried rice to half of an egg crêpe and then fold the other half over. Repeat with the remaining fried rice and crêpes. Garnish with the scallions and serve immediately with the Chile Ketchup on the side.

Modern Mandu

Mandu is a Korean dumpling and a must-have, whether eaten as a snack with a cold beer, or as part of a 20-course meal during a Korean cultural celebration. We love to steam, boil, pan-fry, and even deep-fry these little gems. This recipe is a twist of my late grandmother's northern-style dumplings, which are made primarily from meat with very little filling. To take it up a notch, I add my special pork rillette to the filling.

MAKES: ABOUT 40 DUMPLINGS
PREP TIME: 45 MINUTES
COOK TIME: 10 MINUTES

Mandu Filling:
¼ cup green cabbage
¼ cup bean sprouts
1 pound ground pork
½ cup Ginger Pork Rilette (opposite page)
2 eggs
¼ cup scallions, chopped
1 tablespoon garlic, minced
1 teaspoon garlic powder
1 teaspoon salt
½ teaspoon white pepper
2 tablespoons soy sauce
1 tablespoon sesame oil

1 package Gyoza wrappers (available in Asian markets)
1 egg, beaten with 2 tablespoons water
2 to 3 tablespoons canola oil
¼ cup water to steam each batch of dumplings

1 Place the cabbage in a pot of boiling water over high heat for 25 to 30 minutes. Drain, squeeze out extra water and chop finely. Repeat with the bean sprouts and cook for 25 minutes.

2 Place the soft-boiled cabbage and bean sprouts in a large mixing bowl and add all the other Mandu filling ingredients. Mix well.

3 Drop 1 teaspoon of filling in the center of 1 gyoza wrapper. Lightly brush some egg wash around half the perimeter of the wrapper and fold in half to make a dumpling. Seal tight along the edges with your fingertips, making sure there are no open gaps and place on sheet pan lined with parchment paper. Repeat until all the filling and wrappers have been used. (Makes about 40 dumplings total.)

4 Place the sheet pan of dumplings in the freezer for 20 to 30 minutes. This will help the dumplings to hold their shape during cooking.

5 Place a 12-inch nonstick skillet over medium-high heat. Add enough canola oil to coat the bottom of the skillet and warm for 1 minute. Place 10 to 12 dumplings in the skillet at a time. Sear on the first side for 2 to 3 minutes, or until golden brown. Turn over and immediately add ¼ cup water and cover. Reduce the heat to low and steam for 4 to 5 minutes, or until the water has evaporated. Transfer to a serving platter and repeat with the rest of the dumplings.

6 Serve immediately with the Pimento-Scallion Glaze (page 16) or the Jalapeño Ponzu (page 12) on the side.

Ginger Pork Rilette

My version of pork rilette yields a smooth velvet-like texture. This also makes a great holiday gift, packaged beautifully in a glass jar tied with a pretty ribbon. Just make sure to keep it refrigerated.

MAKES: 6 CUPS
PREP TIME: 4 HOURS
[BUT YOU ARE NOT PREPPING FOR 4 HOURS?]
COOK TIME: 4 HOURS

¼ cup plus 1 cup sesame oil
5 to 6 garlic cloves, minced
4 tablespoons minced fresh ginger plus one 2-inch piece, peeled and sliced in ¼-inch discs
1 tablespoon salt
1 teaspoon white pepper
1½ pounds pork butt
1 cup olive oil
1 cup pork fat (available at your local butcher)

1 Combine the ¼ cup sesame oil, garlic, minced ginger, salt and white pepper in a small mixing bowl to make a paste.

2 Generously rub the pork butt all over with the paste. Place in a glass baking dish or an airtight container coverd with plastic wrap. Refrigerate for at least 3 to 4 hours, or preferably overnight.

3 When you are ready to cook the pork, preheat the oven to 325°F.

4 Place the pork butt in a deep baking dish and top with 1 cup each of sesame oil and olive oil and the pork fat. Cover the baking dish with aluminum foil and bake for 3 to 4 hours, or until fork tender. Remove from the oven and let cool.

5 In a food processor, combine the rilette with some of its cooked liquid and the ginger slices and process until you have achieved a coarse pâte-like texture.

6 Use immediately, or store in an airtight container for up to 10 days in the refrigerator.

Bite-Size Bulgogi Burgers

Nowadays, I don't know anyone who does not love sliders—and everyone enjoys my special twist to the All-American classic. I guarantee that if you make these little guys, you will have an empty platter every time! Ask your butcher to slice the steak and grind rib-eye scraps to make the ground beef.

**SERVES: 8 AS AN APPETIZER,
4 AS AN ENTREE
PREP TIME: 20 MINUTES
COOK TIME: 40 MINUTES**

½ pound rib-eye steak,
sliced deli-thin

½ cup Ginger-Soy Marinade
(page 24)

1 cup Coke or other cola

1 pound ground rib-eye steak

Sea salt and black pepper to taste

Vegetable oil or steak fat, for
seasoning grill

2 slices gouda, quartered

2 tablespoons butter, melted

8 brioche slider buns, or
Hawaiian dinner rolls

8 bamboo toothpicks

For Balsamic-Soy Onions:

1 tablespoon olive oil

1 red onion, julienned

2 tablespoons soy sauce

2 tablespoons balsamic vinegar

Salt and black pepper to taste

For Kimchee Aïoli:

¼ cup mayonnaise

2 tablespoons Classic Napa
Kimchee, drained and finely
chopped (page 34)

2 teaspoons seasoned rice wine
vinegar

1 teaspoon minced garlic

2 tablespoons sesame oil

Sea salt and white pepper to taste

1. In a medium mixing bowl combine the rib-eye steak, Ginger-Soy Marinade, and cola. Cover with plastic wrap and refrigerate for at least 30 minutes.

2. Meanwhile, make the Balsamic-Soy Onions: Heat a medium skillet over medium-high heat. Add the olive oil and warm for 1 minute. Add the red onion and sauté for 2 to 3 minutes. Add the soy sauce, balsamic vinegar, and salt and pepper and stir to combine. Reduce the heat to medium-low and let the onions caramelize until they attain a shiny sugary texture. Remove from the heat and set aside.

3. Next, make the Kimche Aïoli: In a food processor, combine the mayonnaise, Napa Kimchee, vinegar, and garlic. Pulse and then drizzle in the sesame oil. Season with salt and pepper. Transfer to a bowl and set aside.

4. Form 8 hamburger patties with the ground rib-eye, about ½ inch larger than the diameter of the brioche buns. Season with salt and pepper on both sides and heat an outdoor grill or grill pan over medium-high heat.

5. Cook the marinated rib-eye steak on the grill or grill pan, turning constantly with a spatula, for 4 to 5 minutes. Transfer to a bowl and cover with aluminum foil to keep warm. Scrape any residue from the grill with a grill brush and season it again for the beef patties.

6. Cook the beef patties on one side for 2 minutes. Season with salt and pepper. Flip over and place a piece of gouda on each patty. Cook for another 2 to 3 minutes, until the burgers reach desired doneness and the cheese has melted. Remove from heat and let rest.

7. Using a pastry brush, butter both sides of the brioche buns with the melted butter. Toast on the grill for 1 to 2 minutes before assembling the burgers.

8. On the bottom bun, spread a dollop of Kimchee Aïoli, and then place a patty on top. Slather with some Balsamic-Soy Onions and add some rib-eye steak. Spread another dollop of the Kimchee Aïoli on the top half of the brioche bun and place the bun on top of the steak. Repeat to create 8 burgers in all. Spear each burger with a bamboo toothpick through the middle. Transfer to serving platter and serve immediately.

Chapter Eight

From the Sea: My Fish Favorites

My mom tells me that when she was a little girl beef was so sparse. *Galbee*, grilled beef short ribs, were a real treat, reserved for special occasions. Instead her family ate a lot of fish, since it was more readily available. She remembers fishing with my late grandfather and her brother. My grandfather always caught the best fish for my grandmother and she prepared it for dinner. Like most kids, I was not so fond of fish. But then I tried my grandmother's seafood dishes. Just a simple pan-fried yellow corvina never tasted so good as when served with a bowl of rice and some of her homemade *banchan*.

As I got older, I started exploring all the different applications in which we use seafood in Korean cooking. From fish cakes (I offer a recipe for shrimp cakes pan-fried in an egg and flour batter here) or our version of fish sticks (see the catfish recipe in this chapter), there are always several delectable seafood dishes to choose from at a Korean pub. They are typically quick to make and loaded with layers of flavor. All you need is a bowl of rice and you are happy as a clam . . . (no pun intended, of course)!

Spicy Stir-Fried Squid

Another Korean pub standby to enjoy after several bottles of *soju* is this dish we call *ojinguh bokkum*. The sweet spicy sauce wok-tossed with fresh squid and vegetables is always a crowd pleaser. The spicier the dish, the more you tend to drink. If you are not a fan of squid, you can always substitute shrimp or scallops. It's the sauce that makes this dish memorable and addicting. Serve this stir-fry over hot brown rice, soba noodles, or even some spaghetti.

SERVES: 4
PREP TIME: 20 MINUTES
COOK TIME: 20 MINUTES

2 tablespoons sesame oil

1 medium yellow onion, sliced

2 carrots, peeled and sliced into ¼-inch rounds on the diagonal

1 pound squid, cleaned and cut into rings and tentacles

Sea salt and white pepper to taste

1 cup Spicy Chile Slurry (page 62)

¼ Napa cabbage, sliced across into ½-inch strips

2 tablespoons chopped scallions, green parts only, for garnish

1 Heat a wok or large nonstick skillet over medium-high heat. Add the sesame oil and let warm for 1 minute. Add the onions and sauté for 3 to 4 minutes. Add the carrots and sauté for a few minutes more.

2 Add the squid and sauté for 3 to 4 minutes, stirring constantly using the back of a wok ladle. Season with salt and white pepper.

3 Add the Spicy Chile Slurry and cook for a few minutes, stirring to make sure the squid and vegetables are well coated.

4 Add the cabbage and cook for a few more minutes until it's slightly wilted. Taste and adjust the seasoning if needed. Transfer to a serving platter and garnish with the scallions. Serve immediately.

Pan-Fried Halibut

Sangsun jeon (aka "pan-fried fish") is another delicious yet simple fish dish. I remember helping my grandmother dredge the fish in the flour and then watching her fry it to a beautiful golden brown. The light, crisp egg coating makes the fish taste even more buttery. You can choose any white fish you like but I prefer halibut, as its texture is meaty and holds together nicely when cooking. This is a great dish to make with kids to get them involved in the cooking process . . . you may even turn out the next celebrity chef!

SERVES: 4
PREP TIME: 5 MINUTES
COOK TIME: 15 MINUTES

½ cup all-purpose flour

1 teaspoon garlic powder

1 teaspoon onion powder

1 teaspoon sea salt

¼ teaspoon white pepper

2 large eggs, beaten

2 tablespoons sesame oil

1 pound halibut filet, sliced into four 1-inch-thick pieces

1 cup Pimento-Scallion Glaze (page 16)

½ bunch chives, chopped into ½-inch straws, for garnish

1 tablespoon black sesame seeds, for garnish

1 In a shallow pie dish or mixing bowl, combine the flour, garlic and onion powders, sea salt, and white pepper. Mix well and set aside.

2 Preheat the oven to 400°F. Place the beaten eggs in another shallow bowl.

3 Heat a large nonstick skillet over medium-high heat. Add the sesame oil and warm for 1 minute. Reduce the heat to medium.

4 Dredge each fish piece in the flour mixture and lightly shake excess off. Then dip in the egg batter and place in the skillet. Pan-fry the fish on each side for 2 to 3 minutes or until golden brown.

5 Transfer to a sheet pan and bake for 6 to 8 minutes or until cooked through to your liking.

6 Lay the fish flat on a serving platter. Top each piece with 1 tablespoon of the Pimento-Scallion Glaze and garnish with the chives and sesame seeds. Serve immediately, with extra Pimento-Scallion Glaze on the side.

Jeon-Style Shrimp Cakes

Korean pubs always offer an assortment of savory pancakes as they are great for snacking. These little cakes are perfect appetizers for a house party as well. *Jeon* means anything dredged in egg and flour—shrimp, pork belly, or even vegetables—then pan-fried. This version of shrimp cakes combines the flour and egg in the batter. You can substitute sea bass, halibut, or even scallops for the shrimp.

SERVES: 8 TO 10 AS AN APPETIZER, 4 AS AN ENTREE
PREP TIME: 15 MINUTES
COOK TIME: 10 MINUTES

1 pound rock shrimp, coarsely chopped

1 egg

½ cup scallions, white parts only, julienned

1 teaspoon minced garlic

1 teaspoon garlic powder

1 teaspoon onion powder

½ teaspoon sea salt

¼ teaspoon white pepper

2 tablespoons sweet rice glutinous flour (*chapsal*)

2 tablespoons vegetable oil

Pimento-Scallion Glaze (page 16)

2 tablespoons chopped chives, for garnish

1 In a medium mixing bowl, combine the shrimp, egg, scallions, garlic, garlic and onion powders, sea salt, and white pepper. Mix well and then add the rice flour to bind, stirring well so it doesn't clump.

2 Heat a large nonstick skillet over medium-high heat. Add the vegetable oil and heat for 1 minute. Reduce the heat to medium and add dollops of the shrimp mixture (about 2 tablespoons each) to the pan, taking care to leave at least 1 inch in between. The cakes should be about ½ inch thick. Cook them on each side for 3 to 4 minutes or until they are golden brown and the shrimp is cooked through.

3 Transfer the cakes to a serving platter and garnish with the chives. Serve immediately with the Pimento-Scallion Glaze on the side.

Wok-Tossed Fish Cakes

These tasty little cakes are often one of the *banchan* (side dishes) at a Korean BBQ. Even at room temperature, the texture of the tempura holds up nicely in the seasonings. These are also a great starter snack at a pub with an ice cold beer. These fish cakes come in all different shapes and colors, so you can really have fun with this dish. Just be careful when adding salt, as the fish cakes are already packed with flavor.

SERVES: 4
PREP TIME: 5 MINUTES
COOK TIME: 10 MINUTES

2 tablespoons sesame oil

½ medium yellow onion, sliced ¼ inch thick

1 red bell pepper, julienned

1 teaspoon soy sauce

Sprinkle of granulated sugar

1 package fish cake tempura, sliced ¼ inch thick (available in Asian markets)

Sea salt and white pepper to taste

1 tablespoon roasted and salted sesame seeds, for garnish

1   Heat a wok or large nonstick skillet over medium-high heat. Add the sesame oil and warm for 1 minute.

2   Add the onion and sauté for 2 to 3 minutes, or until starting to brown.

3   Add the bell pepper, sauté for 1 minute, then add the soy sauce, sugar and fish cakes. Toss well and cook for another 2 to 3 minutes. Season with salt and white pepper.

4   Transfer to a serving bowl. Garnish with the sesame seeds and serve hot or at room temperature.

Ssam-Style Seafood Sashimi Trio

A typical grab-and-go lunch at a Korean café is *hwae dup bap,* or sashimi rice with a spicy sauce. The freshness of the raw fish mixed with the warm rice, seasonal veggies, and chile sauce is such a delight, especially on a hot day. Nowadays you can find this dish at your local drinking house, as the younger waistline-watching generation, always looking for lighter pub fare options. I take this one step further and present the spicy rice and fish mixture in Korean lettuce wraps. Hence *ssam* style in the recipe title, which means "wrapped in lettuce." If you want to forgo the carbs altogether, you can eliminate the rice from this recipe and make it all about the sashimi-grade fish, which you can find at any good fish store.

SERVES: 8
PREP TIME: 15 MINUTES
COOK TIME: 10 MINUTES

2 cups cooked Calrose rice, hot

2 tablespoons seasoned rice wine vinegar

2 tablespoons mirin

Sprinkle of granulated sugar

½ pound sashimi-grade ahi tuna, diced

½ pound sashimi-grade salmon filet, diced

½ pound sashimi-grade halibut filet, diced

½ cup chopped chives

¼ cup Gochujang Vinaigrette (page 44)

Sea salt and white pepper to taste

1 head romaine lettuce, washed and leaves separated

½ cup *Ssamjang* (page 74)

½ cup Spicy Pickled Cucumbers (page 31)

2 sheets roasted seaweed (*nori,* available in Asian markets) crumbled, for garnish

2 tablespoons tobiko caviar (available at your local fish store), for garnish

2 tablespoons salted and roasted sesame seeds, for garnish

1 In a medium mixing bowl, combine the hot rice, rice vinegar, mirin, and sugar. Mix well with a spoon. Set aside and let cool for a few minutes.

2 In another medium mixing bowl, combine all the fish, the chives, and Gochujang Vinaigrette and mix well. Season with salt and white pepper. Mix well again.

3 On a large flat surface, lay out 8 large lettuce leaves, outsides facing down. Spread 1 teaspoon of the *Ssamjang* in the middle of each lettuce leaf cup.

4 Add a small scoop of the rice mixture (about ¼ cup) to the middle of each leaf cup. Top each with 2 tablespoons of the fish mixture.

5 Evenly distribute the Spicy Pickled Cucumbers among the lettuce leaves, then garnish with the nori, tobiko caviar, and sesame seeds. Serve immediately.

The Other Southern Catfish, Seoul Style

As an American southern gal, I used to look forward to catfish Fridays at the house. My mother would fry up some catfish in true soul-food style, along with collard greens, cornbread, and dirty rice. It was the only fish I looked forward to eating when I was young. She would get out her cast-iron skillet, load it up with an inch of shortening, and let that seafood sizzle. I later discovered that a lot of Korean pubs also fry fish in small nuggets or filets, then serve it with a soy dipping sauce. So, as an ode to my mom and her catfish Fridays, I created this play on the perfect fried-fish snack. You also can turn this into a quick fried-fish sandwich: just add a buttered French roll, lettuce, and sliced tomato. However you choose to eat it, make sure you enjoy this fish while it's hot!

SERVES: 4
PREP TIME: 10 MINUTES
COOK TIME: 15 MINUTES

1 cup all-purpose flour

1 teaspoon garlic powder

1 teaspoon onion powder

1 teaspoon sea salt

¼ teaspoon white pepper

3 eggs, beaten

2 cups panko breadcrumbs

1 teaspoon smoked paprika

1 teaspoon finely ground chile powder (*gochugaru*)

1 pound catfish filets, sliced into 8 pieces

Vegetable oil, for deep frying

2 tablespoons chopped scallions, green parts only

½ cup Kimchee Aïoli (page 90)

1 In a large shallow pie dish or bowl, combine the flour, garlic and onion powders, sea salt, and white pepper. Set aside.

2 Place the beaten eggs in another shallow dish. In a third large shallow pie dish or bowl, combine the panko breadcrumbs, smoked paprika, and chile powder. Set aside.

3 In a large stockpot or cast-iron skillet, heat 3 inches of vegetable oil to 350°F, as measured on a candy or deep-fry thermometer.

4 Dredge each fish piece in the flour mixture, dip into the beaten eggs, and then roll in the breadcrumb mixture to coat.

5 Place the breaded filets in the hot oil and deep-fry for about 5 to 6 minutes, turning a few times, until the fish is cooked through and golden brown on the outside.

6 Transfer the fish to a serving platter. Garnish with the scallions and serve the Kimchee Aïoli on the side for dipping.

Roasted Black Cod with Pimento-Chile Sauce

As you probably have already guessed, we love our chile and spice. I think their heat is a natural complement to some chilled *soju* or an ice-cold beer. We also have an affinity for one-pot dishes like this cod recipe, which is on the top-three bestseller list at any Korean pub. If you visit a mom-and-pop joint, be prepared to consume the whole fish. My gramps would first go for the eyeballs and then work his way to the head. He believed that if you ate the eyeballs first, you would have good vision for a lifetime. Not so sure about the vision thing . . . but if you dare, roast and eat the entire fish. I also recommend serving this family style, along with a big bowl of hot brown rice.

SERVES: 4
PREP TIME: 5 MINUTES
COOK TIME: 30 MINUTES

1 pound black cod filet, skin on

Sea salt and white pepper to taste

2 tablespoons sesame oil

1 small Korean daikon, peeled and cut in quarters lengthwise

8 to 10 Korean peppers (*gochu*)

1 cup Pimento-Scallion Glaze (page 16)

1 yellow onion, sliced ¼ inch thick

2 cups Dashi Stock (page 147)

1 teaspoon chile pepper flakes (*gochugaru*)

¼ cup chopped scallions, for garnish

1 tablespoon roasted and salted sesame seeds, for garnish

Steamed brown rice, for serving

1   Preheat the oven to 350°F. Season the fish filet with sea salt and white pepper.

2   Heat a large nonstick skillet over medium-high heat. Add the sesame oil and let warm for 1 minute. Reduce the heat to medium.

3   Place the filet skin side down on the pan and sear for 3 to 4 minutes or until the skin becomes a nice crusty golden brown. Turn the filet over and sear for another 3 to 4 minutes. Transfer to a roasting pan.

4   Surround the fish with the daikon and Korean peppers. Top the fish with the Pimento-Scallion Glaze and then with the onion slices. Carefully pour the fish stock into the bottom of pan, making sure not to pour it on top of the fish. Cover with aluminum foil and roast in the oven for 20 to 25 minutes or until the fish and vegetables are done.

5   Remove from the oven and let rest for a few minutes. Place the fish in the middle of a serving platter and surround it with the vegetables. Ladle some of the sauce on top and garnish with the scallions and sesame seeds. Serve immediately with brown rice.

Chapter Nine

Savor the Soy: Tantalizing Tofu Dishes

Like most Asian diets, Koreans veer toward a lot of vegetables, grains, and also tofu on a regular basis. My mother used to tell me that tofu, or *dubu*, was considered a steak when she was a young girl. To this day, my mother must cook with it at least a few times a week. It can be used in something as simple as some pan-fried tofu steaks to serve as a protein with your meal—or a spicy stir-fry with kimchee and vegetables, both of which I offer in this chapter. I know that a lot of my friends were never keen on this wonderful soy product until I showed them all the applications in which it could be used. Plus it's good for you and really is a delight to cook with. I hope that my recipes will entice you to savor the soy as much as I do.

Pan-Fried Tofu Steaks with Crispy Anchovies

This is one of the most common staple dishes that Koreans serve at the dining table—and for good reason. For one, it takes minutes to make. And two, it is tasty combined with some rice and kimchee for a quick meal. My grandmother always kept some dried anchovies in her freezer so she could pan-fry them real quick for one of her *banchan* dishes. Just make sure to get the tiny anchovies, as they are ready-to-use and have a sweeter flesh. The larger ones should be reserved for stocks and flavoring soups or stews.

SERVES: 4
PREP TIME: 10 MINUTES
COOK TIME: 10 MINUTES

One 16-ounce package extra-firm tofu, cut into half triangles

¼ cup soy sauce

2 tablespoons sesame oil

½ teaspoon garlic powder

Sea salt and pepper to taste

2 tablespoons vegetable oil, for frying

For Crispy Anchovies:

3 tablespoons sesame oil

½ cup small dried anchovies (*bokum maeruchi*)

4 Korean peppers (*gochu*), sliced into ¼-inch-thick rings

1 teaspoon minced garlic

2 tablespoons soy sauce

Pinch of granulated sugar

1 tablespoon roasted and salted sesame seeds, for garnish

1 Lay the tofu steaks on paper towels to drain excess water.

2 Meanwhile, make the Crispy Anchovies: Heat a medium nonstick skillet over medium heat. Add the sesame oil and warm for 1 minute. Add the anchovies and sauté for a few minutes, stirring constantly. Add the peppers and garlic. Continue to sauté for another 3 to 4 minutes. Add the soy sauce and sugar. Remove from the heat and set aside.

3 In a small mixing bowl, combine the soy sauce, sesame oil, garlic powder, and salt and pepper. Whisk well and set aside.

4 Heat a large nonstick skillet over medium-high heat. Add the vegetable oil and let warm for 1 minute. Reduce heat to medium.

5 Dip the tofu in the soy mixture and then place each piece in the skillet. Cook on each side for 2 to 3 minutes.

6 Transfer to a serving platter. Top each tofu steak with a little of the anchovies. Garnish with the sesame seeds and serve hot or at room temperature.

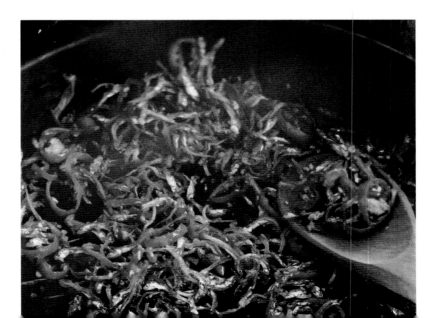

Tofu Stew

Whenever I take my friends to one of my local pubs, at least one of them will order the *doenjang chigae* (aka tofu stew). Basically you can consider it a version of a Korean miso-style stew. It's all about drinking the sweet fermented bean broth and pouring some over the rice. Although this dish can be made without any meat, I think the flank steak adds another flavor dimension and makes it a more satisfying meal.

SERVES: 6
PREP TIME: 15 MINUTES
COOK TIME: 45 MINUTES

2 tablespoons sesame oil

1 yellow onion, sliced ¼ inch thick

2 tablespoons minced garlic

½ pound flank steak, sliced into thin stir-fry strips

2 quarts Dashi Stock (page 13)

¼ cup Korean miso paste (*doenjang*)

2 tablespoons soy sauce

3 tablespoons granulated sugar,

One 16-ounce package firm tofu, cut into 1-inch cubes

Sea salt and black pepper to taste

1 bunch scallions, green parts only, julienned, for garnish

Cooked Calrose rice, for serving

1 Heat a large stockpot over medium-high heat. Add the sesame oil and warm for 1 minute. Add the onion and sauté for 1 minute. Add the garlic and sauté for a few minutes. Add the beef and brown for 3 to 4 minutes, stirring constantly.

2 Add the Dashi Stock and bring to a boil. Reduce the heat to a medium-low simmer, cover and cook for about 20 minutes. Add the *doenjang*, soy sauce, and sugar. Reduce the heat to a low simmer and cook for another 10 minutes.

3 Add the tofu and cook for a few minutes. Season with salt and pepper. Remove from the heat.

4 To serve, divide equally between 6 large soup bowls. Garnish with the scallions and serve immediately with steamed white rice on the side.

Soybean Sprout Soup

Once you sit down at your table at a Korean pub, the waitress will bring you a pot of complimentary soup. At one pub in particular you always get their version of *kongnamul guk* (aka soybean sprout soup). It's a nice palate teaser that, for whatever reason, really gets you hungry. My friends will always order second and third helpings of this soup, and sometimes even take a bowl home for the next day. The soybean sprouts give it a light nutty flavor and it has such a clean finish. Make a batch and keep this in the refrigerator as your go-to soup when you are craving a little snack.

SERVES: 6
PREP TIME: 20 MINUTES
COOK TIME: 1 HOUR

2 tablespoons sesame oil

1 yellow onion, sliced ¼ inch thick

3 tablespoons minced garlic

½ pound pork butt, sliced into thin stir-fry strips

1 quart Dashi Stock (page 147)

1 pound soybean sprouts, cleaned and bottom ends trimmed (available in Asian markets)

3 tablespoons Korean miso paste (*doenjang*)

2 tablespoons soy sauce

1 tablespoon finely ground chile powder (*gochugaru*)

Sea salt and white pepper to taste

4 red Korean peppers (*gochu*), sliced into rings, for garnish

1 Heat a large stockpot over medium-high heat. Add the sesame oil and warm for 1 minute. Add the onion and sauté for 1 minute. Add the garlic and sauté for a few minutes. Add the pork and brown for 3 to 4 minutes, stirring constantly.

2 Add the Dashi stock and bring the soup to a boil. Add the soybean sprouts and reduce the heat to a medium-low simmer. Cover and cook for about 30 minutes.

3 Remove the lid and add the miso paste, soy sauce, and chile powder. Reduce the heat to a low simmer and cook for another 10 to 12 minutes. The soybean sprouts should be cooked and tender. Season with salt and white pepper.

4 Remove from the heat. To serve, divide equally between 6 serving bowls. Garnish with the Korean peppers and serve immediately.

Chilled Tofu with a Scallion Salsa

One of the best things about tofu is that it can be found in almost every supermarket and it's ready to eat. Whether you want to top your favorite salad with it or drop some in a tortilla to make your own vegan taco—you don't have to cook it. Here's my version of a cold vegan-friendly dish that I love to order when out on a hot summer night. It also makes a great accompaniment to one of the heavier pub fares that you may order. Make sure to drain the tofu on layers of paper towels for at least 30 minutes so that you really can taste the flavor of the cold tofu.

SERVES: 4
PREP TIME: 15 MINUTES
COOK TIME: 5 MINUTES

½ cup Pimento-Scallion Glaze (page 16)

1 hot-house cucumber, diced

½ cup Korean daikon, diced

½ small red onion, diced

Sea salt and white pepper to taste

One 16-ounce package extra firm tofu, cut into half triangles, drained and patted dry

3 tablespoons sesame oil

2 tablespoons chopped scallions, for garnish

1 tablespoon roasted and salted sesame seeds, for garnish

1 In a medium mixing bowl, combine the Pimento-Scallion Glaze, cucumber, daikon, and red onion. Mix well, then season with salt and pepper.

2 Arrange the tofu flat on a large serving platter. Top each tofu steak with a rounded teaspoon of the salsa and drizzle with the sesame oil.

3 Garnish with the scallions and sesame seeds and serve cold.

Stir-Fried Tofu with Kimchee and Seasonal Vegetables

It's rare that I meet someone that does not appreciate a delicious stir-fry. Especially when you add a kick to it with some homemade kimchee (I prefer to use the classic napa kimchee). It really elevates the standard tofu stir-fry, giving it some great heat and flavor. Eat this solo or opt for some nutty steamed brown rice.

SERVES: 4
PREP TIME: 15 MINUTES
COOK TIME: 10 MINUTES

2 tablespoons sesame oil

½ small red onion, julienned

1 carrot, peeled and julienned

1 cup Classic Napa Kimchee (page 34), cut into ½-inch slices

1 green bell pepper, julienned

¼ cup Dashi Stock (page 147)

1 tablespoon red chile bean paste (*gochujang*)

2 tablespoons soy sauce

One 16-ounce package extra-firm tofu, cut into 1-inch cubes

Sea salt and white pepper to taste

1 bunch scallions, green parts only, julienned, for garnish

Cooked brown rice, for serving (optional)

1   Heat a wok or large nonstick skillet over medium-high heat. Add the sesame oil and warm for 1 minute.

2   Add the onion and sauté for a few minutes. Add the carrot and continue to sauté. Add the Kimchee and bell pepper and saute for a few more minutes. Add the Dashi Stock and red chile bean paste, then reduce the heat to medium.

3   Add the soy sauce and tofu. Toss well, making sure to coat the tofu and vegetables with the sauce. Season with salt and white pepper.

4   Transfer to a deep serving platter or large pasta bowl. Garnish with the scallions and serve immediately with steamed brown rice, if you like.

Chapter Ten

The Chicken or the Egg: My View of the Bird

My mother told me that when she was young she rarely ate chicken—it was seen as a poor man's food in Korean culture. I thought that was so strange, as some of my fondest food memories as a kid involve chicken! But, as times change, so do customs. When my grandparents moved to America in the late seventies, my grandmother became obsessed with fried chicken. She would sneak out to eat fast-food chicken constantly, devouring the breading with gusto. My mom was guilty of driving her to get a bucket of good old KFC from time to time, and I guess you could say I went along for the ride . . .

Well my grams was not the only Korean who caught on to the delicious trend of fried chicken. Every restaurant in K-town now offers chicken *bulgogi*, a Korean fried chicken, and even some sort of chicken stew or *jim*. The irony of it all: Preparations that my mother said were considered peasant fare back in the day have become some of the most popular items on Korean menus today. It's so good to know that tastes have evolved with the times. As a Korean-American, I can't imagine my life without eating chicken on a weekly basis. I consider it one of those universal proteins that can be used in so many ways. I have included recipes for some of my favorite chicken—and egg—dishes, which you can also find in most local Korean cafés and pubs. These are perfect for a quick family dinner at home, bringing a genuine sense of comfort to all who partake. After all—who doesn't love a great bird?

Korean Fried Chicken

Your first bite into this succulent version of a twice-fried bird will change your concept of breadless chicken forever. Traditionally referred to as *tong dak*, the recipe typically calls for a whole chicken, and you are served half a fried chicken along with pancakes, pickled daikon, and various dipping sauces. When developing this recipe for my food truck, I wanted to make it a little easier to consume on the streets, so I stuck to chicken drumsticks, which are more in line with the American conception of fried chicken. The crispiness of the crackling skin, the result of frying the chicken twice, gives it that bacon-esque quality. Bite into your first leg and you will be a convert for good!

SERVES: 6
PREP TIME: 15 MINUTES
COOK TIME: 25 MINUTES

Vegetable oil, for deep frying

12 large chicken drumsticks, skin on

1 cup Pickled Daikon (page 29)

For Roasted Garlic-Soy Glaze:

1 cup Chicken Stock (page 147)

1 cup brown sugar

1 cup soy sauce

1 cup mirin

2 cups roasted garlic cloves, puréed

2 tablespoons chopped scallions, for garnish

1 tablespoon roasted and salted sesame seeds, for garnish

1 In a deep stockpot, heat 6 to 8 inches of vegetable oil until it reaches 375°F when measured with a candy or deep-fry thermometer. Add the drumsticks and fry for about 8 minutes. Transfer to a cookie sheet and set aside, reserving the oil in the stockpot.

2 In a medium saucepan, combine all ingredients for the Roasted Garlic Soy–Glaze and bring to a low boil over medium heat. Simmer for 20 to 25 minutes, or until the sauce has reduced by a third. Remove from the heat and set aside.

3 Heat the reserved oil until it reaches 375°F again. Fry the drumsticks again, for 4 to 5 minutes, or until cooked through. Insert a meat thermometer into the thickest part of the leg; when the temperature reads 160°F, the chicken is done. Transfer immediately to the saucepan of Roasted Garlic–Soy Glaze and let sit for about 2 minutes to allow the chicken to absorb the flavors.

4 Shake the excess glaze off and transfer the chicken thighs to a serving platter. Sprinkle with the chopped scallions and sesame seeds and serve immediately.

Soju-Braised Chicken

Some of my favorites one-pot dishes are stews. Especially during the winter, there is nothing quite like the comfort of a stew with a rich broth—and the fact that the second day of this meal is always better than the first. One of my favorite stews is *dak jim*, or "chicken in the pot." It's a spinoff of the classic *galbee jim*, a short-rib stew that we typically eat on holidays and special occasions. I prefer the chicken version as it is lighter and tastes great over some hot steamed rice or buttermilk mashed potatoes. I've even cheated by serving this meal at home and then reheating it the next day for a small dinner party with friends. A nice crusty baguette or buttermilk biscuits to sop up this addicting broth is a welcome addition. Serve this stew with a simple salad and you have an amazing dinner—two days in a row!

SERVES: 4, PLUS LEFTOVERS
PREP TIME: 10 MINUTES
COOK TIME: 1½ HOUR

8 chicken leg quarters, skin on

1 quart Ginger-Soy Marinade (page 24)

2 tablespoons sesame oil

1 quart Chicken Stock (page 147)

One 375-ml bottle *soju* (available in Asian markets)

2 yellow onions, quartered

1 pound new potatoes, cleaned

½ pound baby carrots

Sea salt and white pepper to taste

¼ cup chopped scallions, for garnish

1 In a large mixing bowl, combine the chicken and Ginger-Soy Marinade. Cover with plastic wrap and refrigerate for at least 30 minutes.

2 Heat a large stockpot over medium-high heat. Add the sesame oil and warm for 1 minute. Reduce the heat to medium and add the chicken legs, skin side down. Sear for 3 to 4 minutes, or until a nice golden brown crust forms. Add the chicken stock, *soju*, and remaining marinade from the mixing bowl. Bring to a medium boil and then reduce to a medium-low simmer. Cover and cook for about 20 minutes.

3 Add the onions, potatoes, and carrots. Cover and cook for another 40 minutes.

4 Check for doneness with a fork: The chicken and potatoes should be fork-tender and cooked through. Season with salt and white pepper. Remove from the heat and let sit for about 5 minutes with the cover on.

5 Serve in 4 pasta bowls, placing 1 chicken leg quarter in each bowl. Add a few potatoes, pieces of onions, and carrots to each serving. Finally pour at least ½ cup of the broth over each piece of chicken. Garnish with the scallions and serve immediately. Refrigerate leftover stew for another meal.

Grilled Chicken Gizzards

Like most Asian cultures, Koreans tend to use all parts of an animal in our cooking. My father is a fan of the neck of any animal—and always looks forward to eating the neck bones of the turkey on Thanksgiving morning. My mother, on the other hand, is a gizzard fan. As a child, I was not too keen on the idea of eating gizzards, but when I grew older and started frequenting Korean drinking houses, I noticed that most of the menus included gizzards. I tried them and fell in love. The sweet soy glaze in this recipe makes these grilled gizzards a treat. Add a bowl of rice with some kimchee and you will be a happy camper. I would also recommend serving these with udon or ramen on a cold winter night.

SERVES: 4 TO 6
PREP TIME: 5 MINUTES
COOK TIME: 30 MINUTES

1 pound chicken gizzards, rinsed under cold water and patted dry
½ cup soy sauce
1 cup mirin
Sea salt and white pepper to taste
Soy-Mirin Glaze (page 21)
Chicken fat to season grill
1 tablespoon roasted and salted sesame seeds, for garnish

1   In a medium mixing bowl, combine the gizzards, soy sauce, and mirin, and season with salt and white pepper. Cover with plastic wrap and refrigerate for about 30 minutes.

2   Meanwhile, prepare the Soy-Mirin Glaze.

3   Season an outdoor grill or grill pan with the chicken fat and heat to medium-high heat. Remove the gizzards from the refrigerator and place on the hot grill. Cook for 3 to 4 minutes, then turn over and cook for another 3 to 4 minutes. Brush with a little glaze and continue to turn every 2 minutes, brushing with glaze each turn, until the gizzards are cooked through.

4   Transfer to a serving platter. Drizzle with extra marinade and sprinkle with the sesame seeds. Serve immediately.

Chile Chicken Wings

I am the first to admit that whenever I go to a bar, chicken wings are one of the first things I look for on the menu. You could say I am a wing connoisseur—I will devour anything from a basic buffalo version to a Thai wing stuffed with shrimp. There is something so magical in these little meaty drummettes. It's one of those universal appetizers that lends itself to so many different flavor variations. I always appreciate a spicy wing, especially with a cold beer. My chile-spiced wings will be a hit at parties—whether you're throwing a luncheon, cocktail party, or Super Bowl bash. Licking of the fingers is optional, but highly recommended.

SERVES: 6 TO 8
PREP TIME: 5 MINUTES
COOK TIME: 40 MINUTES

2 pounds chicken drummettes, skin on

Vegetable oil, for deep frying

Sea salt and white pepper to taste

For Soju Chile Sauce:

1 cup red chile bean paste (*gochujang*)

½ cup soy sauce

½ cup rice vinegar

¼ cup honey

¼ cup mirin

2 tablespoons brown sugar

2 tablespoons coarse chile pepper flakes (*gochugaru*)

One 375-ml bottle *soju* (available in Asian markets)

½ cup minced garlic

1 teaspoon salt

1 teaspoon white pepper

1 tablespoon black sesame seeds, for garnish

1 tablespoon roasted and salted sesame seeds, for garnish

1 First, make the Soju Chile Sauce: In a medium saucepan, combine all the ingredients and mix well. Bring to a low boil and then lower the heat and simmer, stirring occasionally, for 20 minutes.

2 Preheat the oven to 400°F.

3 In a large stockpot, heat 6 to 9 inches of vegetable oil until it reaches 375°F as measured on a candy or deep-fry thermometer. Add the wings and cook for 5 to 6 minutes, or until lightly golden. Transfer to a mixing bowl.

4 Season with salt and white pepper. Pour the chile sauce over the wings and toss well, making sure to coat each wing thoroughly. Transfer to a roasting pan and bake in the oven for 6 to 8 minutes, or until the wings are cooked through.

5 Transfer to a serving platter and garnish with both kinds of sesame seeds. Serve immediately.

Making the Perfect Egg Omelet

There is such beauty in the perfect square omelet. It is definitely an art form in both Korean and Japanese cuisine. We call it a million-layer omelet. Once you get the technique down, you will have officially entered the Korean hall of fame.

The Tools
To make the perfect egg omelet, it is essential for you to purchase a square nonstick omelet pan at your local Asian grocery store. In addition, make sure to buy the extra-long chopsticks with very thin tips. This will allow you to gracefully lift the crêpe.

Step 1: Making Your First Layer
Pour a thin layer of egg mixture and spread it by gently tilting the pan to cover the surface like you would a crêpe. Cook over low heat, making sure the omelet does not burn.

Step 2: Rolling Your Omelet
Using the tip of your chopsticks, lift the far side of the crêpe and carefully roll it toward you.

Step 3: Repeating Step 2
Continue to roll the crêpe and build upon the omelet, creating a jelly-roll shape.

Step 4: The Final Product
You have now perfected the art of the Korean egg omelet!

The Ultimate Egg Omelet

Like most Americans, the younger Korean generation craves breakfast at midnight. The first time I ate at a Korean pub, my friends ordered an omelet. When it came to the table, we all thought: "That's it?" Little did we know how creamy and sweet this simple yet divine egg creation could be. The trick is in the layering of the omelet during cooking, so I have included instructions and photos to guide you. It sounds like a lot of effort for an omelet, but once you take a bite and it melts in your mouth, it's worth every bit. Serve this day or night, with some hot white rice and Spicy Pickled Cucumbers, if you like.

MAKES: 1 OMELET
PREP TIME: 5 MINUTES
COOK TIME: 10 MINUTES

3 large eggs
3 tablespoons heavy cream
1 tablespoon mirin
1 teaspoon granulated sugar
¼ teaspoon sea salt
Pinch of white pepper
1 tablespoon vegetable oil
1 tablespoon chopped scallions, green parts only, for garnish

1   In a small mixing bowl, combine all the ingredients except the vegetable oil and garnish. Whisk well and set aside.

2   Heat a square nonstick omelet pan over medium-high heat. Add the vegetable oil and warm for 1 minute. Reduce the heat to medium.

3   Add a splash of cold water to the egg mixture and whisk well. Pour a quarter of the egg batter on the pan, making sure it covers the surface like a thin crêpe. With the extra-long chopsticks, lightly lift the layer, slowly rolling it into a jelly-roll shape.

4   Repeat step 3 three more times, continuing to build upon the jelly-roll until all the egg batter is cooked, about 10 minutes.

5   Transfer to a plate, garnish with the scallions, and serve immediately.

Chicken Curry Turnovers

Most Asian cultures have some sort of traditional curry. The spiciness and richness of these sauces or stews are always so satisfying. Typically Koreans eat our curry over rice or perhaps with a hamburger patty or pork cutlet. Once, when I was putting together a cocktail party at home, I took some of my leftover curry and made a turnover with it. Turned out it was the hit of the night—everyone was asking for the recipe—so I thought it was only fair to share it here. You can use any leftover curry for the filling, no matter the protein; all you need is a little puff pastry. I even suggest freezing these turnovers to use as appetizers for last-minute entertaining. They also are popular after-school snacks for the kids. What's not to love when it involves a flaky, buttery crust?

**MAKES: 16 TURNOVERS
(8 SERVINGS)
PREP TIME: 20 MINUTES
COOK TIME: 1½ HOURS**

1 tablespoon sesame oil

½ yellow onion, diced

½ pound chicken breast, cut into ½-inch cubes

2 cups Chicken Stock (page 147)

1 carrot, peeled and diced

1 russet potato, peeled and cut into ½-inch cubes

½ package Korean curry paste blocks (available in Asian markets)

¼ cup frozen peas

½ cup Greek yogurt

Sea salt and white pepper to taste

1 package puff pastry sheets, slightly thawed

2 eggs, beaten with 3 tablespoons water

1 Heat a large stockpot, over medium-high heat. Add the sesame oil and warm for 1 minute. Add the onions and brown for a few minutes. Add the chicken and brown for another 3 to 4 minutes, stirring constantly with a wooden spoon. Add the Chicken Stock, carrot, and potato. Cover and simmer for 20 minutes over medium-low heat.

2 Add the curry paste and cook for 5 minutes, stirring occasionally to make sure it has dissolved. Add the peas and fold in the yogurt. Cook for another 2 to 3 minutes. Season with salt and white pepper.

3 Remove from the heat and spread on a sheet pan. Chill the curry in the refrigerator for at least 30 minutes.

4 Preheat the oven to 325°F. Grease a cookie sheet. Cut the puff pastry sheets into sixteen 4 x 4-inch squares.

5 Remove the curry from the refrigerator. Place 2 tablespoons curry in the middle of each puff pastry square. Fold the pastry over the filling on a diagonal, making a triangle. Using a fork, press down on the edges to seal. Repeat until you have 16 turnovers. Brush each turnover with the egg wash.

6 Arrange the turnovers on the prepared cookie sheet and bake for 12 to 15 minutes, or until the pastry is crisp and golden brown. Using a spatula, transfer the turnovers to a serving tray. Serve immediately.

Chapter Eleven

The Green Garden: Vegetarian Delights

I think one of the most amazing things about Korean cuisine is the endless array of vegetable dishes. It's rare that we eat an all-protein meal because, as my mother always said, you need to cut through some of the heaviness of the meat with a vegetable dish or two. Sometimes on a hot summer day when our family wanted to eat light, my mother made an all-veggie dinner with some steamed rice and a few Korean pickles on the side. She called it her "Green Garden Buffet." I think it was her way to get my brother and I excited about eating vegetables. It worked—ever since I was a little girl I have loved eating vegetables.

Even at a pub late at night, I always order a few vegetable plates. They are full of flavor and add just the right balance to your meal. Living in Los Angeles, I have several vegetarian and vegan friends, and one of their favorite cuisines to eat is Korean, as there are always so many vegetarian and vegan choices just off a *banchan* bar in a local Korean supermarket.

I hope these dishes inspire you and your family to load up on what my mother refers to as "the 4-cup rule": She always made sure we had 4 cups of fresh cooked vegetables a day. Not a bad rule, I must say. You can serve any of these recipes as a side dish alongside a roast chicken or grilled steak. Or perhaps choose three or four of your favorites and make it a veggie night, rounded out with steamed brown rice and a bowl of Spicy Pickled Cucumbers.

Fried Eggplant, Seoul Style

Every Asian cuisine serves some version of eggplant. It's one of my favorite vegetables and I always order it when I see it on a menu, whether it's a traditional Italian eggplant Parmesan or a Thai eggplant stir-fried with basil and lots of chiles. Koreans tend to use the Japanese eggplant because its small size is convenient for cooking, and it has a sweeter flavor than the classic eggplant we find in most supermarkets. The skin is not as thick, which makes it more tender and easier to work with. This recipe is one of the most simple but delicious ways to enjoy eggplant. Serve it as a first course or as a side with a grilled steak. It is foolproof and even the kids will love it.

SERVES: 4 TO 6
PREP TIME: 5 MINUTES
COOK TIME: 10 MINUTES

8 Japanese eggplants, tops cut off
¼ cup Korean Miso-Honey Glaze (page 19)
Sea salt
Vegetable oil, for deep frying
1 tablespoon roasted and salted sesame seeds, for garnish

1 In a deep stockpot or cast-iron skillet, heat 1½ inches of vegetable oil to 350°F as measured on a candy or deep-fry thermometer.

2 Drop the eggplant in the hot oil and cook for 2 to 3 minutes on each side. Transfer to a tray lined with paper towels to absorb excess oil.

3 Sprinkle with sea salt while still hot. Transfer the eggplant to a serving platter and drizzle with the Korean Miso-Honey Glaze. Sprinkle with the sesame seeds and serve immediately.

Sesame Squash Stew

Hobak chigae is a traditional summer squash stew that is made with a Korean miso broth. *Hobak*, or Korean summer squash, looks similar to a very round and light green zucchini. The meat of the squash is sweet and best during the summer months. However, you can easily substitute zucchini or yellow squash. This refreshing summer stew is just the thing to serve for a casual dinner or late-summer lunch with friends. All you need is some steamed rice and you are all set.

SERVES: 4
PREP TIME: 5 MINUTES
COOK TIME: 20 MINUTES

2 tablespoons sesame oil

1 medium yellow onion, sliced in thin strips

1 pound Korean squash, washed, sliced in half lengthwise, and cut into ½-inch slices

Sea salt and white pepper to taste

1 quart Veg Stock (page 146)

3 tablespoons Korean miso paste (*doenjang*)

2 tablespoons soy sauce

1 tablespoon granulated sugar

2 tablespoons chopped scallions, green parts only, for garnish

Steamed Calrose or brown rice, for serving

1 Heat a medium stockpot over medium-high heat. Add the sesame oil and warm for 1 minute. Reduce the heat to medium. Add the onions and cook for 2 to 3 minutes until translucent. Add the squash and cook for 2 to 3 minutes longer until translucent. Season with salt and white pepper.

2 Add the vegetable stock, turn up the heat to medium-high, and bring to a rolling boil. Reduce the heat to medium and simmer the stew for about 5 minutes. Stir in the miso paste, soy sauce, and sugar. Cover and simmer for another 10 minutes. Season with salt and white pepper if needed.

3 Remove from the heat and divide equally among 4 soup bowls. Garnish with the scallions and serve immediately with steamed white or brown rice on the side.

Buttered King Oyster Mushrooms

Whenever I go to the Korean supermarket, I love to head to the produce section and taste the samples. There is normally a sweet lady who is handing out some soy buttered mushrooms. This is a quick version of buttered mushrooms that we normally see at a steak house. I prefer king oyster mushrooms as they are very meaty in texture. A splash of soy sauce makes this recipe so much better. Serve these royal funghi with a chicken breast for a quick mid-week meal or a grilled steak for a no-hassle weekend barbecue with friends.

SERVES: 4
PREP TIME: 5 MINUTES
COOK TIME: 10 MINUTES

2 tablespoons sesame oil

3 tablespoons unsalted butter

1 pound king oyster mushrooms, sliced ¼ inch thick

2 tablespoons minced garlic

Splash of soy sauce

Sea salt and white pepper to taste

2 tablespoons chopped chives, for garnish

1 Heat a large nonstick skillet or wok over medium-high heat. Add the sesame oil and warm for 1 minute. Reduce the heat to medium. Add the butter and mushrooms and sauté for 3 to 4 minutes, stirring constantly. Add the garlic and toss well. Cook for another 2 to 3 minutes. Add a splash of soy sauce and season with salt and white pepper. Cook for another minute or two.

2 Transfer to a serving bowl. Sprinkle with the chives and serve immediately.

Grilled Korean Pumpkin

Korean pumpkin is what you may refer to as kabocha squash. I asked my mother when I was young, "Why do we call a squash a pumpkin?" She told me she thought it was because of its shape and orange flesh. The flavor of kabocha squash is also similar to that of a pumpkin, but they are normally smaller in size. I suggest getting a smaller one for this dish, as it is easier to slice and clean. This is a great side dish to serve with grilled pork chops. The sweetness of the squash makes it a good substitute for the roasted apples often served with pork. In the fall, grilled pumpkin typically appears as a special on restaurants menus.

SERVES: 4 TO 6
PREP TIME: 10 MINUTES
COOK TIME: 15 MINUTES

½ cup soy sauce

½ cup mirin

2 tablespoons sesame oil

1 small kabocha squash, skin on, sliced into ½-inch wedges

Sea salt and white pepper to taste

1 tablespoon black sesame seeds, for garnish

1 Preheat an outdoor grill or grill pan to smoke point and brush it with vegetable oil.

2 In a large mixing bowl, combine the soy sauce, mirin, and sesame oil. Whisk well. Add the squash and toss thoroughly, making sure all the pieces are coated with the marinade.

3 Place the squash on the grill and season with salt and white pepper. Cook for 4 to 5 minutes and then turn over. Cook on the other side for another 4 to 5 minutes or until fully cooked.

4 Transfer to a serving platter and sprinkle with the sesame seeds. Serve immediately.

Roasted Sweet Potatoes with a K-town Kick

During my first visit to Seoul, my grams handed me a skewer of beautiful candied potatoes. Here, I take inspiration from that dish but add a smoky and spicy kick. Serve with grilled salmon or a roast chicken.

SERVES: 4
PREP TIME: 10 MINUTES
COOK TIME: 45 MINUTES

2 large sweet potatoes, peeled and cut into ½-inch dice

¼ cup sesame oil

3 tablespoons soy sauce

1 tablespoons granulated sugar

1 teaspoon garlic powder

1 teaspoon finely ground chile powder (*gochugaru*)

1 teaspoon smoked paprika

Sea salt and white pepper to taste

1 tablespoon roasted and salted sesame seeds, for garnish

1. Preheat the oven to 400°F. Grease a baking dish.

2. In a large mixing bowl, combine the sweet potatoes, sesame oil, soy sauce, sugar, garlic and chile powders, and smoked paprika, tossing to make sure the sweet potatoes are well coated. Season with salt and white pepper.

3. Transfer to the prepared baking dish. Cover with aluminum foil and bake for 15 minutes.

4. Remove the foil and give the sweet potatoes a good stir. Bake for another 15 minutes and stir again. Check for doneness by using a fork to spear a sweet potato. If it's tender, the sweet potatos are cooked.

5. Transfer to a serving bowl. Sprinkle with the sesame seeds and serve hot immediately.

Shiitake Chicharones

When I created my meatloaf recipe (page 84), I was looking for some added crunch. My Japanese sous chef threw dried shiitake mushrooms in the deep fryer. The flavor reminded me of *chicharones*, the fried pork skin that I love, without the guilt about all the fat.

SERVES: 4
PREP TIME: 10 MINUTES
COOK TIME: 45 MINUTES

8 ounces dried shiitake mushrooms, soaked in hot water

Smoked Chile Salt (page 135)

Vegetable oil, for deep frying

1. Drain the mushrooms and squeeze out excess water. On a cutting board, julienne each mushroom, making paper-thin slices. Wrap in a paper towel and squeeze out excess water again. Set aside.

2. Heat 3 inches vegetable oil in a wok or cast-iron skillet until it reaches a temperature of 350°F when measured with a candy or deep-fry thermometer.

3. Drop the mushrooms into the hot oil. Using a skimmer, separate the mushrooms so they fry evenly. Cook for 4 to 5 minutes or until nicely golden brown. Remove from the heat and strain well.

4. Transfer to a serving bowl, sprinkle with the Smoked Chile Salt, and toss well. Serve immediately or store in an airtight container for 2 days.

Smoky Fried Peppers

Talk about a taste-bud teaser! Korean peppers are similar to Japanese shishito peppers, though not as wrinkled on the outside. They pack a little more heat when raw, but when cooked they tend to become mild and smoky. I enhance the flavor of these wonderful little bites with my own smoked chile salt. Instead of a bowl of chips, put out a plate of these for impromtu guests and you will be crowned the queen of the ball!

SERVES: 8 to 10
PREP TIME: 5 MINUTES
COOK TIME: 10 MINUTES

Vegetable oil, for deep frying
1 pound Korean or shishito peppers

For Smoked Chile Salt:
2 tablespoons sea salt
1 teaspoon finely ground chile powder (*gochugaru*), or ½ teaspoon cayenne pepper
1 teaspoon smoked paprika

1 First, make the Smoked Chile Salt: In a large mixing bowl, combine all the ingredients.

2 In a deep stockpot, place 4 inches of vegetable oil and heat until it reaches 375°F when measured with a candy or deep-fry thermometer.

3 Add the peppers and fry them for 3 to 4 minutes. Once you see the skin of the peppers start to crackle, transfer immediately to the large mixing bowl with the Smoked Chile Salt and toss well.

4 Transfer to a serving bowl and serve immediately.

Chapter Twelve

Drink and Be Merry!
Korean-Inspired Cocktails

Now that you have learned all of my favorite pub grub, it is vital that you don't forget what the food is supposed to pair with . . . a cocktail of course! Typically when you go to a drinking house, you have your choice of *soju* (the Korean twist on vodka, though a bit sweeter in taste, available in Asian markets), beer, and scotch or whiskey. Although traditionally you are supposed to drink your liquor straight up, unfortunately, I do not have that kind of tolerance. Ever since the late nineties, *soju* has turned up in all kinds of restaurants where it features in a margarita, martini, and even a gimlet. I decided to take it to the next level and merge some great fruits with the typical choices of liquor Koreans may veer to.

Since Korean fare tends to be on the spicy and salty side, I selected some sweet cocktails you can enjoy with your friends. These are fun for entertaining, or even when you have something special to celebrate with your family. It's worth it to invest in a cocktail shaker and a muddler. Most importantly, make sure to toast: Raise your glass and say *"GUN BAE!"* every time you take a sip and you will have officially experienced Korean pop culture.

Ginger Gimlet

I have always loved a great gimlet. The flavor of the muddled mint paired with gin is so refreshing. So that got me thinking about using fresh ginger instead. The freshness of muddled ginger is great and adds a unique twist to the traditional cocktail. I love serving this with my ginger beef skewers (page 24) or Soju-Braised Chicken (page 118).

MAKES: 1 COCKTAIL
PREP TIME: 5 MINUTES

2 ounces vodka
½ ounce lime juice
½ ounce simple syrup

1 small slice of fresh ginger
1 lime wheel for garnish
Rocks glass, filled with ice cubes

1   In a martini shaker, muddle the ginger. Add the vodka, lime juice, and simple syrup. Shake well and strain into the glass filled with ice.

2   Garnish with the lime wheel and serve immediately.

Magnolia Mojito

When thinking about what to flavor this cocktail with, I immediately turned to magnolia berry syrup. Available in Korean bakeries or online, this syrup is typically used in tea. The fruit syrup and mint meld nicely with this drink, and cut through the spice of my *tteokboki* (page 62) or Chile Chicken Wings (page 120).

MAKES: 1 COCKTAIL
PREP TIME: 5 MINUTES

3 to 4 slices lime
8 to 10 mint leaves, plus 1 sprig for garnish
1½ ounce light rum

2 ounces magnolia berry syrup
1½ ounces simple syrup
2 ounces soda
Collins glass, filled with ice cubes

1   In a martini shaker, muddle the lime and mint leaves together. Add the rum, magnolia berry syrup, simple syrup, and soda. Shake well and strain into the glass filled with ice.

2   Garnish with the mint sprig and serve immediately.

Seoul-Style Sour

My brother's favorite drink is a whiskey sour, so I decided to give it a little K-town flair by adding the slightly carbonated yogurt drink you can find in most Asian markets. Its sour flavor really gives it a unique taste. Pair with my Pork Belly with Soy-Mirin Marinade (page 21) or Mama Lee's Meatloaf (page 84).

MAKES: 1 COCKTAIL
PREP TIME: 5 MINUTES

Rocks glass
2 key lime wheels, cut in quarters, plus 1 wheel for garnish

1 ounce Jack Daniels
2 ounces sweet-and-sour mix
2 ounces Yakin yogurt drink

1   Fill the glass with ice cubes and the lime quarters.

2   Pour in the Jack, then the sweet-and-sour mix, and finally the yogurt drink.

3   Garnish with the lime wheel and serve immediately.

Pusan Punch (aka the Korean Mai Tai)

This is my take on the traditional Mai Tai. The combination of tropical juices makes this a terrific complement to several of my dishes, particularly the chicken meatballs (page 83). I have added a drop of magnolia berry syrup to add some floral accents, making this a gorgeous cocktail to show off when entertaining.

MAKES: 1 COCKTAIL
PREP TIME: 5 MINUTES

Collins glass
1 ounce light rum
1 ounce guava juice or nectar
1 ounce mango juice or nectar
1 ounce pineapple juice
1 ounce mandarin orange juice or tangerine juice
1 ounce magnolia berry syrup (available at Korean bakeries or online)
1 ounce Meyer's dark rum
1 pineapple wedge, for garnish
2 tablespoons fresh mango, diced, for garnish

1 Fill the glass with ice cubes. Add the light rum and then the guava juice.

2 Carefully pour the mango, pineapple, and mandarin juices, one at a time, along the side of the glass so that the various colors float, creating layers.

3 Pour the magnolia berry syrup into the middle of the drink so it floats to the bottom of the glass.

4 Top with the dark rum for a floater.

5 Garnish with the pineapple wedge and diced mango and serve immediately.

Soju Sangria

I don't know anyone who doesn't love sangria. For some reason, it just puts you into party mode and gets you ready to celebrate. I had a white sangria back in the day that made me think how tasty a version with *soju* would be. The addition of aloe vera juice and tropical fruits make this a delight. I highly suggest making this the day before, so the fruits have time to steep with the *soju*. Serve with an array of my skewers (see chapter 1, page 10) or the Jeon-Style Shrimp Cakes (page 98). It will keep the day light and full of flavor.

MAKES: 1 COCKTAIL
PREP TIME: 5 MINUTES

½ cup grapes, cut in half

½ cup diced Korean pear (*shingo*, available in Asian markets)

½ cup diced mango

½ cup diced plum

One 375-ml bottle of *soju*

One 8-ounce can aloe vera juice (available in Asian markets)

1 ounce Grand Marnier

2 ounces simple syrup

1 lime, cut into lime wheels and then quartered, plus 4 wheels, for garnish

Wine glasses

1. In a large container with an airtight lid, combine all the ingredients except the garnish. Mix well and cover. Refrigerate for at least a couple of hours, if not overnight.

2. Transfer to a serving pitcher and pour into the wine glasses. Garnish with lime wheels.

The Korean Royale

It is customary for a Korean to bring a bottle of Crown Royal to a house party; we consider it the universal bottle to toast and celebrate with. Like I said before, I don't have the stomach to drink such a strong liquor straight up, so I decided to come up with a cocktail using it. I added some rice punch, a drink made with brown sweet rice, cinnamon, and pine-nut tea, and a splash of the Korean carbonated yogurt drink to make it complete. Serve this with Bossam-Style Steamed Pork Belly (page 74) or Hangover Stew (page 73).

MAKES: 1 COCKTAIL
PREP TIME: 5 MINUTES

Rocks glass

Brown sugar, to coat the glass rim

1 ounce Crown Royal

1 ounce Yakin yogurt drink (available in Asian markets)

2 ounces rice punch (available in Asian markets)

1 Wet some paper towels and place the mouth of the glass on top.

2 On a small plate, spread a layer of brown sugar. Place the mouth of the glass on top of the sugar to create a rim.

3 Fill the glass with ice cubes.

4 Add the Crown Royal, then the yogurt drink, and then the rice punch. Serve immediately.

Seoultown Sunrise

Back in the day, my thing was to wake up in the mornings, head to the beach, and have a tequila sunrise with my brunch. I don't know why I only ordered it with brunch—as it goes well with a lot of other dishes during the day. Tequila is also one of those liquors that tastes terrific with Korean food. All the spice, garlic, and salt really plays well with a tequila-inspired cocktail. My version of this citrus concoction swaps out the OJ with some mandarin and pineapple juice. The Grand Marnier floater really completes it. Serve it with my Spam and Eggs (page 77) or my fried catfish (page 101). You won't be sorry!

MAKES: 1 COCKTAIL
PREP TIME: 5 MINUTES

Collins glass

1½ ounces tequila, preferably Patron

4 ounces mandarin orange juice

1 ounce pineapple juice

Splash Grand Marnier

1 orange slice, for garnish

1 Fill the glass with ice cubes. Add the tequila, then both juices. Float a splash of Grand Marnier.

2 Garnish with the orange slice and serve immediately.

Makegeolli Martini

Makgeoilli, the original rice wine of Korea, is an unfiltered wine beverage with floral accents that make it truly unique. I decided to make a martini out of the official drink of our country, adding some fruit to complement the wine. Make no mistake: *Makgeolli* is as potent as vodka or gin so pour wisely. Pair this cocktail with my Spicy Chilled Buckwheat Noodles (page 44) or the traditional *Pajeon* (page 56). Or serve as an aperitif before dinner to get those taste buds going.

MAKES: 1 COCKTAIL
PREP TIME: 5 MINUTES

2 ounces *makgeolli*
2 ounces muscat juice
1 ounce apple schnapps
5 to 6 red grapes, sliced, for garnish
Martini glass

1 Fill a martini shaker with 1 cup of ice cubes. Add the *makgeolli*, muscat juice, and schnapps.

2 Cover with the lid and shake well. Strain and pour into the glass.

3 Garnish with the grapes and serve immediately.

The K-town Malt

There is one Korean tradition that I do like to keep: having some scotch at the end of my meal. The sweetness of the scotch really ends a meal quite perfectly, and it is a great digestif. I like to chase it with a little cola so it's not as strong. So, in keeping with tradition, I decided to modernize a perfect ending to a perfect meal.

MAKES: 1 COCKTAIL
PREP TIME: 5 MINUTES

1 ounce *soju*
2 ounces scotch
1½ ounces simple syrup
4 ounces Coke or other cola, chilled
Rocks glass

1 Fill the glass with the *soju*, scotch, and simple syrup. Using a small spoon, mix well.

2 Add the cola and serve immediately.

The Basics

My goal in writing this book is not only to share the wonderful flavors and stories that Korean cuisine has to offer, but to demystify the notion that Asian food is difficult to prepare. It's all about the basics, as my grams used to say. Although Korean food is complex in flavor, it is simple when you break down the methods of preparation, and I've broken them down into pantry, stocks, and technique sections.

The Pantry

To make cooking easier, I suggest keeping a pantry stocked full of my go-to items. Most are shelf friendly and keep for a long while. Once you become familiar with these ingredients, you can incorporate them into some of your own favorite recipes.

Finely Ground Sea Salt

Not only is this finely ground sea salt great for cooking, it is what we use to pickle all our vegetables. It is extremely economical in Korean and Asian grocery stores and typically comes in a 1- to 2-pound bag.

White Pepper

White pepper is very common in Asian cuisine, especially in Korean cooking. The heat from the white peppercorn yields a slightly different flavor and aroma than that of the black peppercorn. For freshness, it's best to buy the peppercorns whole and grind them in your coffee grinder as needed.

Salted and Roasted Sesame Seeds

These are a staple garnish and flavoring in almost every Korean dish. You can find them in the spice aisle at Korean markets and some Japanese grocery stores, as well. The seeds are mixed with salt and partially ground during roasting (see page 150 to make your own). Store them in an airtight container in the refrigerator for 1 month.

Coarse Chile Pepper Flakes (*Gochugaru*)

This is the staple chile pepper seasoning of our cuisine. Made from the pimento pepper, the seeds are ground along with the skins of the pepper with extremely hot results. It is the kind of heat that creeps up on you during your last bite! Coarse chile pepper flakes are used for pickling and also for stocks and sauce bases. Store in your refrigerator in an airtight container, for up to 60 days.

Finely Ground Chile Powder (*Gochugaru*)

A powdered version of the coarse chile pepper flakes, this finely ground seasoning is used most commonly for salads, meat rubs, and soups. A little goes a long way with this smoky fiery chile. Store in your refrigerator in an airtight container for up to 60 days.

Red Chile Bean Paste (*Gochujang*)

The Korean version of ketchup, this red chile paste is used as a stir-fry sauce, in soups, salads, and more. It is also used as a condiment for dipping Asian-style crûdité such as cucumbers and daikon. The sweet spicy flavor is delicious in a marinade for pork or chicken or added to your favorite fried rice dish. Store in an airtight container in your fridge for up to 6 weeks.

Fermented Soybean Paste (*Doenjang*)

Known as the Korean miso, this paste is a little more concentrated than that of a typical white Japanese miso. The hearty flavor is good for sauces, stocks, stews, and soups. Store in an airtight container in your refrigerator for up to 8 to 10 weeks.

Seasoned Rice Wine Vinegar

Our staple vinegar we use for salads, marinades, and more, seasoned rice wine vinegar can be found at most supermarkets in the Asian food aisle. Store in a cool dark place for up to 4 months.

Sesame Oil

There is nothing quite like the fragrant aroma of toasted sesame oil. It is the base oil that we use for marinades, salads, and general cooking. I prefer either the Korean or Japanese brands of sesame oils, as the quality of the press is much higher.

Soy Sauce

The most common flavoring in Korean cooking, soy sauce should be stored in an airtight container in a cool dry place. I do not recommend refrigerating your soy sauce, as you will lose some of that delicious salt-brewed flavor. If properly stored, it can be kept for up to 6 months.

Salted Baby Shrimp (*Saewoojut*)

Primarily used as a salting agent, these baby shrimp are typically used in pickling our various kimchees. In addition, we use the shrimp to flavor a steamed egg custard and for stocks and stews. I suggest using a little at a time, as the salt content of these mini crustaceans is extremely high. Store in an airtight glass jar in your refrigerator for up to 6 months.

Baby Dried Anchovies (*Bokum maeruchi*)

These dried anchovies are a staple of our *banchan* (side dishes) and are most commonly stir-fried. Perfect as a snack over some hot rice and kimchee, the salty sweet essence of this dried fish is a delightful contribution to the Korean cupboard. Store in an airtight plastic bag in your freezer for up to 6 months.

Large Dried Anchovies (*Dashi maeruchi*)

These larger-sized anchovies are primarily used as a flavoring ingredient in stocks and soups and should not be eaten out of hand as a snack. Once submerged in liquid for longer than 30 minutes, the dried fish tends to take on a bitter taste. Store in an airtight plastic bag in your freezer for up to 6 months.

Sweet Dried Japanese Seaweed Sheets (*Kombu*)

This sweet seaweed, found in Japanese waters, is great as a flavoring agent for stocks, stews, and soups. However, do not allow the *kombu* to cook for longer than 20 minutes, or it will yield a bitter aftertaste. *Kombu* can be found in Korean supermarkets and most Asian grocery stores. Store in an airtight plastic bag in the freezer for up to 3 months.

Dried Shiitake (Black Chinese) Mushrooms

These meaty dried mushrooms are great for flavoring your favorite sauce or soup. I prefer using the dried version over fresh as the flavor is much more pronounced. They can be found in most markets these days. Store in an airtight plastic bag in a cool dark place for up to 1 month.

Buckwheat Noodles (*Naeng myun*)

This stretchy and somewhat elastic version of Korean soba is most commonly used in a cold summer noodle soup and a spicy chilled buckwheat noodle dish. This nutty and chewy noodle comes either dry or frozen at your local Korean supermarket. If you use the frozen version, make sure to thaw the noodles at room temperature and pull apart the strands before boiling.

Sweet Glutinous Rice Flour (*Chapsal*)

Used as a binding agent for pancakes and other common Korean batters, *chapsal* is made from a sweet glutinous rice flour. Add it in the very last stage of preparing your batter to prevent clumps from forming. Store in an airtight plastic bag in a cool dark place for up to 3 months.

Korean peppers (*Gochu*)

Our daily pepper, which we consume raw, cooked, and even pickled, is similar in shape to the long thin Japanese shisito pepper but the skin is not as wrinkled and a much more rich vibrant dark green like a jalapeño pepper. Like Anaheim chiles, these peppers are medium hot. Since these are fresh, they can be stored in the refrigerator for up to 1 week in an airtight plastic bag.

Calrose Rice (*Bap*)

This short-grain and somewhat glutinous rice is light and fluffy in texture. I use it in all my rice dishes. You also may find Calrose in Japanese cuisine, including sushi. For best results, make sure to wash and soak it prior to cooking (see page 149).

Rice Cake Cylinders (*Tteokboki tteok*)

This Korean version of rice gnocchi comes frozen unless you are able to get fresh rice cakes at your local Korean bakery. I always keep a few packs handy in the freezer; they keep for 6 months. See page 151 for prep.

The Stocks

I always keep a few of my favorite stocks in the freezer so I can make a quick stew or soup. Take an afternoon to make a few batches. They are easy to make and freeze and homemade stock improves the flavor of any dish you add it to.

Veg Stock

I have quite a few vegan and vegetarian friends and always want to make sure they're meal-time needs are met. This veg stock is great for sautéeing vegetables, or even boiling your favorite grain or bean. Make a full batch as you will use this by the gallon.

MAKES: 3 QUARTS
PREP TIME: 15 MINUTES
COOK TIME: 1¾ HOURS

1 large Korean daikon, peeled and quartered lengthwise

2 large sweet potatoes (perferably garnets), peeled and cut into quarters

2 large yellow onions (skin on), cut in half

½ cup garlic cloves

1 leek, cut in half

3 carrots, peeled and cut in half

Sea salt and white pepper to taste

Sesame oil, for coating

1 gallon water

1 piece *kombu* (dried Japanese seaweed)

1 Preheat the oven to 325°F.

2 On a large baking sheet, arrange the vegetables so they are evenly distributed. Drizzle with the sesame oil and toss to coat well. Sprinkle with sea salt and white pepper to taste. Roast in the oven for about 40 minutes.

3 Transfer the roasted vegetables to a large stockpot. Add the water, season with sea salt and white pepper, and bring to a rolling boil over medium-high heat. Reduce the heat to medium, cover, and simmer for about 45 minutes. Add the *kombu* and simmer for another 15 minutes. Remove from the heat and immediately discard the *kombu*.

4 Let cool. Strain through a fine-mesh sieve into an airtight container. Store in the refrigerator for up to 1 week or in the freezer for up to 1 month.

Dashi Stock

The most common stock in Korean cuisine, dashi is used in marinades, soups, and stews. Whereas the Japanese make it with bonito, we use anchovies. Make sure to remove them after cooking as they become bitter if left in the stock for too long.

MAKES: 3 QUARTS
PREP TIME: 15 MINUTES
COOK TIME: 2 HOURS

1 large Korean daikon, peeled and quartered lengthwise

2 large sweet potatoes (preferably garnets), peeled and cut into quarters

2 large yellow onions (skin on), cut in half

½ cup garlic cloves

1 leek, cut in half

3 carrots, peeled and cut in half

Sesame oil, for coating

Sea salt and white pepper to taste

1 gallon water

4 ounces large dried anchovies (*dashi maeruchi*)

1 Preheat the oven to 325°F.

2 On a large baking sheet, arrange the vegetables so they are evenly distributed. Drizzle with the sesame oil and toss to coat well. Sprinkle with sea salt and white pepper to taste. Roast in the oven for 40 minutes.

3 Transfer the roasted vegetables to a large stockpot. Add the water, season with sea salt and white pepper, and bring to a rolling boil over medium-high heat. Reduce the heat to medium, cover, and let simmer for about 45 minutes. Add the anchovies and let simmer for another 25 minutes. Remove from the heat and immediately discard the anchovies.

4 Let cool. Strain through a fine-mesh sieve into an airtight container. Store in the refrigerator for up to 1 week or in the freezer for up to 1 month.

Chicken Stock

Other than the dashi stock, this is one of my most used stocks, so I always keep some on hand. If you don't have chicken bones leftover from another recipe, ask the butcher in the meat department of your local supermarket to sell you some. They are cheap and just a few pounds makes an ample supply of stock.

MAKES: 3 QUARTS
PREP TIME: 15 MINUTES
COOK TIME: 2½ HOURS

½ large Korean daikon, peeled and sliced in half

1 large sweet potato (preferably garnet), peeled and cut into quarters

2 large yellow onions (skin on), cut in half

½ cup garlic cloves

1 leek, cut in half

2 carrots, peeled and cut in half

Sesame oil, for coating

Sea salt and white pepper to taste

3 pounds chicken bones

1½ gallons water

1 Preheat the oven to 325°F.

2 On a large baking sheet, arrange the vegetables evenly. Drizzle with the sesame oil and toss to coat well. Sprinkle with sea salt and white pepper to taste. On a separate baking sheet, spread the chicken bones evenly and sprinkle with sea salt and white pepper to taste. Place both trays in the oven. Roast the vegetables for about 40 minutes and the chicken bones for about 1 hour.

3 When each is ready, transfer the roasted vegetables and chicken bones to a large stockpot. Add the water, season with sea salt and white pepper, and bring to a rolling boil over medium-high heat. Reduce the heat to medium, cover, and simmer for about 1½ hours.

4 Let cool. Strain through a fine-mesh sieve into an airtight container and store in the refrigerator for up to 1 week or in the freezer for up to 1 month.

Bone-Marrow Stock

There is nothing quite like a hearty beef bone-marrow stock. I use this in sauces and also some stews. I also whip it out in the wintertime when I want to make a traditional rice cake soup for a last-minute dinner. Make sure to chill this stock overnight before using—and skim off and discard the fat that accumulated to get the most flavor possible.

MAKES: 3 QUARTS
PREP TIME: 15 MINUTES
COOK TIME: 2½ HOURS

1 large Korean daikon, peeled and quartered lengthwise

3 large yellow onions (skin on), cut in half

½ cup garlic cloves

2 leeks, cut in half

3 carrots, peeled and cut in half

Sesame oil, for coating

Sea salt and black pepper to taste

5 pounds beef marrow bones

2 gallons water

6 to 8 dried shiitake mushrooms

1   Preheat the oven to 325°F.

2   On a large baking sheet, arrange the vegetables evenly distributed. Drizzle with the sesame oil and toss to coat well. Sprinkle with sea salt and black pepper to taste. On a separate baking sheet, spread the beef marrow bones evenly and sprinkle with sea salt and black pepper to taste. Place both trays in the oven. Roast the vegetables for about 40 minutes and the beef bones for about 1 hour.

3   When each is ready, transfer the roasted vegetables and the beef bones to a large stockpot. Add the water, season with sea salt and black pepper, and bring to a rolling boil over medium-high heat. Reduce the heat to medium, cover, and simmer for about 1 hour. Add the shiitake mushrooms and simmer for another 30 minutes.

4   Let cool. Strain through a fine-mesh sieve into an airtight container. Store in the refrigerator for up to 1 week or in the freezer for up to 1 month.

Pork Stock

People tend to forget about the wonderful buttery flavor of a well-done pork stock. In Korean cuisine, we love to use it for our favorite stews, as it only enhances the pork pieces in the stew. I suggest using the pork neck bones as they give the best flavor and are always easy to come by at your local butcher.

MAKES: 3 QUARTS
PREP TIME: 15 MINUTES
COOK TIME: 2½ HOURS

1 large Korean daikon, peeled and quartered lengthwise

2 sweet potatoes (preferably garnets), peeled and cut in half

3 large yellow onions (skin on), cut in half

½ cup garlic cloves

2 leeks, cut in half

3 carrots, peeled and cut in half

Sesame oil, for coating

Sea salt and white pepper to taste

5 pounds pork neck bones

2 gallons water

1   Preheat the oven to 325°F.

2   On a large baking sheet, arrange the vegetables evenly. Drizzle with the sesame oil and toss to coat well. Sprinkle with sea salt and white pepper to taste. On a separate baking sheet, spread the pork neck bones evenly and sprinkle with sea salt and white pepper to taste. Place both trays in the oven. Roast the vegetables for about 40 minutes and the pork bones for about 1 hour.

3   When each is ready, transfer the roasted vegetables and the pork bones to a large stockpot. Add the water, season with sea salt and white pepper, and bring to a rolling boil over medium-high heat. Reduce the heat to medium, cover, and simmer for about 1½ hours.

4   Let cool. Strain through a fine-mesh sieve into an airtight container. Store in the refrigerator for up to 1 week or in the freezer for up to 1 month.

The Techniques

Understanding some basic techniques of Korean cuisine is essential to your success—and helps ensure that your homemade pub grub is as delicious (and authentic) as the real deal!

Cooking Rice in a Rice Cooker

Cooking the perfect bowl of rice is key to enrolling in the Korean kitchen. I don't know of any Korean household that does not have a rice cooker, and I recommend that you purchase one, too. It is the best investment: I do everything from cooking rice to steaming vegetables, meat, and even potatoes. Make sure to soak your rice before cooking, as described below, as it allows the rice grains to open in preparation.

Step 1: Washing Rice

Place the rice in the rice cooker bowl and wash it well with warm water. Using your fist, massage the rice to rid it of all the excess powder. Tip the bowl to drain out the water and rinse a few more times.

Step 2: Soaking Rice

Soak the rice in hot water for at least 15 minutes. This prepares the rice grains for cooking. Level off the surface of the rice.

Step 3: Adding Water

Using your index finger as a gauge, place the tip of your finger on the top of the rice and add warm water until you reach the first section of your finger (approximately an inch). Contine to follow cooker instructions.

Drying Out Tofu

One of the biggest mistakes people make when working with tofu is not allowing it to drain of excess water before cooking. Tofu is soy based, but when it's drenched with water, the flavor is lost. Especially when frying tofu or eating it raw, drying it out first will create a much more flavorful dish.

Step 1: Layering Your Towels

Place several layers of paper towels flat on a plate. Lay the tofu on top and let drain for about 10 minutes. Discard the paper towels and any liquid that has gathered on the plate.

Step 2: Flip and Repeat

Using a fresh set of paper towels, turn the tofu over and repeat step 1.

Cleaning Squid

Most cooks are not inclined to clean their own squid, however, it is probably one of the easiest and quickest seafood items to clean. The process takes just a few minutes. Once you get past your fear of the whole squid, you realize what a flavor difference truly fresh squid makes.

THE WHOLE SQUID

The basic anatomy of squid is very easy to understand. There is the head, the body (aka the ring section) and the legs (aka the tentacles). Normally you reserve the body and legs for consumption.

Step 1: Cutting the Head

With a sharp chef's knife, cut off the head right below the neck and discard it.

Step 2: Rinsing the Squid

Turning the body inside out, rinse the squid under cold running water and pull off and discard any excess lining.

Step 3: Cutting the Squid

First cut off the legs and group them into little clumps almost like broccoli florets. Then cut the body into rings about ¼ inch thick, or as instructed in the recipe.

Roasting and Salting Sesame Seeds

Roasted and salted sesame seeds are as readily available at your local Korean market as salt and pepper. In the event that you do not have a Korean market nearby, I have provided a quick breakdown of how to make your own. Personally, I think they are the best homemade!

Step 1: Washing

In cold water, wash your sesame seeds to get rid of any excess powder. Drain well and set aside.

Step 2: Heating

Heat a nonstick skillet over medium-low heat. For every cup of sesame seeds, add 2 tablespoons fine sea salt to the pan. Make sure to evenly distribute the seeds in the bottom of the pan with a wooden spoon.

Step 3: Grinding

Using the end of a wooden pastry roller, grind the seeds slowly, almost like you would with a mortar and pestle. Ideally you want to break open some of the seeds. Lower the heat if necessary, making sure not to burn the seeds. The seeds should reach a light golden brown, about 20 minutes.

Step 4: Final Product

Let the seeds cool completely, then store in an airtight container in the refrigerator for up to 1 month. Use in your favorite marinades, salads, and sauces, and as a garnish in most Korean dishes.

Cooking Buckwheat Noodles

Korean buckwheat, aka *naeng myun*, is similar to a thin and stretchy soba noodle. It tends to be somewhat glutinous in texture so it's important to learn how to handle these delicate nutty noodles.

Step 1: Prepping

Like any Korean noodles, *naeng myun* comes in two forms: frozen or dried. If they are frozen make sure to let the noodles thaw at room temperature. Pull the strands apart so that the noodles do not clump together during cooking.

Step 2: Boiling

Once the noodles have been dropped into boiling water, use a long pair of chopsticks to stir the noodles constantly while cooking, about 3 to 4 minutes for frozen noodles, 7 to 8 for dried. They should be a little chewy and elastic.

Step 3: Rinsing

Immediately place the cooked noodles under cold running water and continue to swirl them with your chopsticks. This will prevent the noodles from clumping together.

Step 4: Drizzling

Drizzle a little sesame oil on the noodles and work it through with your hands to prevent the noodles from sticking together.

Prepping Rice Cakes (Tteok)

Typically you will find rice cakes in the refrigerated section at your local Korean market. Since they are commercially made, I have a few helpful tips to help you take these cylinders apart.

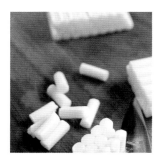

Step 1: Boiling

Leaving the rice cakes in their packaging, drop them in boiling water for a few minutes.

Step 2: Opening

Remove and open the packet immediately with a sharp knife. Be careful as it will be hot.

Step 3: Cutting

Gently pull the cylinders apart and cut each in half, making approximately 1-inch-long cylinders.

Step 4: Final Product

You are now ready to make your favorite rice cake dish!

Sources

Korean Markets

You should be able to find all the special ingredients used in my recipes at the following online sites.

H MART
www.hmart.com/company_new/shop_main.asp

HANNAM CHAIN
www.hannamchain.com/home.php?siteID=6

KOA MART
www.koamart.com

These two sites direct you to store locations.

GALLERIA MARKET/HK MARKET
www.galleriamarket.com/location.html

GREENLAND MARKET
www.greenlandmarket.net

Specialty Korean Markets

This is a great source for magnolia berry syrup.

HOWONDANG
www.howondang.com

Asian Markets

The following online sites are great sources for panko breadcrumbs, mirin, seaweed, soy sauce, and Calrose rice.

ASIAN FOOD GROCER
www.asianfoodgrocer.com

MITSUWA MARKETPLACE
www.mitsuwa.com/english/index.html

Index

Acknowledgments

This book is dedicated to the loved ones who supported my love of food and life. First to the ladies in my family: my mother and late grandmother. Without them I would not carry the spirit of cooking in my soul. Mom, I love you and each time I cook, I think of my favorite childhood memories of being in the kitchen with you. May my late grandmother be smiling from above, knowing that she gave me the gift of her cooking wand. I truly believe that each time I pick up a knife, I carry a part of her with me.

As for the men in my life—Dad, Gramps, and my brother Robbie—you have all been my strength in my success. Dad, you are my rock and no matter the obstacles, you have always believed in my food and talent. You have set an example of a true fighter, and this book is a result of what you have ingrained in me as a child. Thanks to my dear late Gramps, who always told me I had my grandmother's gift and encouraged me to cook for family celebrations. And to my loving brother Robbie, who I look up to as my best friend and one of the best businessmen alive. You have always served as my boxing coach and showed me how to fight until the end, and to always come out on top.

To my right hand and little sis Kelli Bautista. You are truly family and have always stood by me and believed. Not to mention you concoct the best cocktails in town! Thanks for collaborating for the cocktails chapter and making my vision of Korean libations come true. To my business partner and second brother Viet Do. You have always been my #1 fan and protector. You have shown your faith in me from the very first day we rolled out with our food truck. I look forward to many more years of business success and Sunday Suppers!

A huge amount of grattitude goes out to Quentin Bacon, who not only honored me with his photographic talent, but has become a dear friend and foodie. Thank you for taking on this project and making my first cookbook shoot such a memorable one! Special thanks go out to Sienna DeGovia and her amazing culinary team. You have officially become Korean and can whip up kimchee fried rice like nobody's business! A heartfelt thanks to Robin Turk who found the most amazing props and, most importantly, was so gracious to lend us her home for this shoot. I am so happy to have introduced you to the wonders of Korean cuisine.

I would like to thank Kyle Cathie for allowing me to share my love of pub grub with the world. Thanks to my wonderful editor at Kyle Books, Anja Schmidt, and to Ron Longe, for all his hard publicity work. This has truly been an amazing journey and I am so happy to have found a publishing home.

Last and certainly not least, special thanks to my agent and friend, Marisa Bulzone. You made my dream come true, coming back to believe almost 10 years later. Thank you for seeing what I did not, and allowing me to come full circle and find myself as a chef and author. Without you, I would not be writing any of these words. Thanks for believing!